Wide Angle

2

WORKBOOK

OXFORD
UNIVERSITY PRESS

KATE ADAMS

OXFORD
UNIVERSITY PRESS

198 Madison Avenue
New York, NY 10016 USA

Great Clarendon Street, Oxford, OX2 6DP,
United Kingdom

Oxford University Press is a department of the University of Oxford. It furthers the
University's objective of excellence in research, scholarship,
and education by publishing worldwide. Oxford
is a registered trade mark of Oxford University
Press in the UK and in certain other countries

ISBN: 978 0 19 452837 5

Printed in China
This book is printed on paper from certified and well-managed sources.

ACKNOWLEDGMENTS
Back cover photograph: Oxford University Press building/David Fisher
Illustration: A. Richard Allen/Morgan Gaynin Inc, pp. 46.
Video: Mannic Productions, pp. 5, 26, 47.
*The Publishers would like the thank the following for their kind permission to reproduce photographs
and other copyright material:* **123RF:** pp. 67 (public speaking/kasto), 82 (exterior of plane/
Vereshchagin Dmitry), **Alamy:** pp. 4 (Friends/Everett Collection Inc.), 17 (trash/Ian
Allenden), 18 (mowing lawn/Greatstock), 20 (students/Cathy Topping), 30 (people building/
Xinhua), 30 (pinning clothes to a dressform/Ciulture Creative), 37 (farmers' market/
JeffG), 51 (person in bike helmut/Alvey & Towers Picture Library), 51 (burning building/
Rob Potter), 51 (male in car/Lev Dolgachov), 65 (actors theatre/Paul Doyle), 65 (dancers/
theatrepix), 74 (people at exhibit/Derek Hudson), 81 (people hiking/Colby Lysne), **Blink:**
pp. COVER (Edu Bayer), 23 (puppet studio/Gianni Cipriano), 30 (pottery maker/Gianni
Cipriano), 66 (eyewear production/Gianni Cipriano). **Getty:** pp. 6 (colleagues chatting/
Morsa Images), 30 (students in decorating cakes/AleksandarNakic), 31 (male students/
Thomas Barwick), 32 (Robo Thespian/Laura Lezza), 37 (department store/Juanmonino), 37
(hairdresser/Ian Allenden), 44 person receiving award/Caiaimage/Paul Bradbury), 44 (proud
parents/Gary D Ercole), 44 (astonomer/National Geographic/Babak Tafreshi), 44 (female
doctor/Brand X), 45 (reading in park/Kosamtu), 51 (children in costumes/George Doyle),
51 (searching for a missing person/ Mark Wilson), 51 (lifeguard/ Joss Joss), 54 (woman
riding a bike/Aleksandar Nakic), 76 (autograph/Caiaimage/Tom Merton), 80 (orangutan
in rainforest/BAY ISMOYO / Staff), 9 (family/Ariel Skelley), 10 (online (friends/W2
Photography), 39 (person working out/Daniel Grill), 39 (person working out/Daniel Grill),
65 (movie star @ Academy Awards/Kevin Winter), Newscom: pp. 27 (person skateboarding/
CB2/ZOB/WENN.com). Rex: pp. 25 (winner of 2016 Olympic marathon/Sergei Ilnitsky /
Epa). **Shutterstock:** pp. 11 (male co-workers chatting fizkes), 18 (preparing a meal/
Monkey Business Images), 23 (preparing a meal/wavebreakmedia), 23 (balanced meal/
Nitr) 23 (men with coffee cups/wavebreak), 24 (spaghetti/stockphoto-graf), 30 (texting/
Andrey_Popov), 37 (mall/ gracethang2), 38 (interior of a cruise ship/ Ally Lee), 39 (woman
on cruise ship/ Oleksandr Lysenko), 44 (disappointed student/ Antonio Guillem), 44 (couple
getting married/ IVASHstudio), 52 (shelter in woods/PeterJeffreys), 53 (children in costume/
MichaelJung), 60 (computer programmer/ESB Professional), 65 (musicians/Asia Images), 65
(fashion show/ Jade ThaiCatwalk), 73 (room with a view/ Olga Gavrilova).

Authentic Content Provided by Oxford Reference
*The author and publisher are grateful to those who have given permission to reproduce the following
extracts and adaptations or copyright material:*

p.3 Montaigne in *Oxford Essential Quotations* (5th ed.) edited by Susan Ratcliffe. Copyright
Oxford University Press 2017. http://www.oxfordreference.com/view/10.1093/
acref/9780191843730.001.0001/q-oro-ed5-00007567?rskey=Lrftll&result=1

p.3 Thomas Merton in Oxford Essential Quotations (5th ed.) edited by
Susan Ratcliffe. Copyright Oxford University Press 2017. http://www.
oxfordreference.com/view/10.1093/acref/9780191843730.001.0001/q-oro-ed5-
00019805?rskey=p50VEa&result=1

p.7 Mark Zuckerberg in *Oxford Essential Quotations* (5th ed.) edited by
Susan Ratcliffe. Copyright Oxford University Press 2017. http://www.
oxfordreference.com/view/10.1093/acref/9780191843730.001.0001/q-oro-ed5-
00017121?rskey=FvTCXa&result=1

p.10 Adapted from *A Dictionary of Computer Science* (7th ed.) edited by Andrew
Butterfield and Gerard Ekembe Ngondi. Copyright Oxford University Press 2016.

http://www.oxfordreference.com/view/10.1093/acref/9780199688975.001.0001/acref-
9780199688975-e-6468?rskey=akP97Q&result=2

p.14 Sallust in *Oxford Essential Quotations* (5th ed.) edited by Susan Ratcliffe. Copyright
Oxford University Press 2017. http://www.oxfordreference.com/view/10.1093/
acref/9780191843730.001.0001/q-oro-ed5-00009096?rskey=JYxJJe&result=1

p.17 Adapted from *A Dictionary of Economics* (5th ed.) by John Black, Nigar Hashimzade,
and Gareth Myles. Copyright oxford University Press 2017. http://www.oxfordreference.
com/view/10.1093/acref/9780198759430.001.0001/acref-9780198759430-e-1462

p21 Lyndon B. Johnson in *The Oxford Dictionary of American Quotations* (2nd ed.) edited
by Hugh Rawson and Margaret Miner. Copyright Oxford University Press 2008. http://
www.oxfordreference.com/view/10.1093/acref/9780195168235.001.0001/q-author-
00008-00000855?rskey=HqpuYH&result=1

p.24 Adapted from *A Dictionary of Sports Studies* by Alan Tomlinson. Copyright
Oxford University Press 2010. http://www.oxfordreference.com/view/10.1093/
acref/9780199213818.001.0001/acref-9780199213818-e-810?rskey=VPtJb5&result=7

p.28 William Cowper in *Oxford Dictionary of Quotations* (8th ed.) edited by Elizabeth
Knowles. Copyright Oxford University Press 2017. http://www.oxfordreference.com/
view/10.1093/acref/9780199668700.001.0001/q-author-00010-00000830?rskey=1cGwb
F&result=16

p.31 Adapted from *A Dictionary Of Education* (2nd ed.) edited by Susan Wallace. Copyright
Oxford University Press 2015. http://www.oxfordreference.com/view/10.1093/
acref/9780199679393.001.0001/acref-9780199679393-e-1130?rskey=zuLddl&result=1

p.35 Maya Angelou in *Oxford Essential Quotations* (5th ed.) edited by
Susan Ratcliffe. Copyright Oxford University Press 2017. http://www.
oxfordreference.com/view/10.1093/acref/9780191843730.001.0001/q-oro-ed5-
00000286?rskey=J25D9s&result=1

p.38 Adapted from *The Oxford Companion to Ships and the Sea* (2nd ed.) edited by I. C. B.
Dear and Peter Kemp. *Copyright Oxford University Press 2007.* http://www.oxfordreference.
com/view/10.1093/acref/9780199205684.001.0001/acref-9780199205684-e-
719?rskey=rCnfeJ&result=1

p. 42 Ralph Waldo Emerson in *The Oxford Dictionary of American Quotations* (2nd ed.) edited
by Hugh Rawson and Margaret Miner. Copyright Oxford University Press 2008. http://
www.oxfordreference.com/view/10.1093/acref/9780195168235.001.0001/q-author-
00008-000000517?rskey=Shd5Q6&result=1

p.45 Joan Didion in *Oxford Essential Quotations* (5th ed.) edited by
Susan Ratcliffe. Copyright Oxford University Press 2017. http://www.
oxfordreference.com/view/10.1093/acref/9780191843730.001.0001/q-oro-ed5-
00004327?rskey=76v63b&result=1

p.49 Apple Computer Inc. in *The Oxford Dictionary of American Quotations* (2nd ed.) edited
by Hugh Rawson and Margaret Miner. Copyright Oxford University Press 2008. http://
www.oxfordreference.com/view/10.1093/acref/9780195168235.001.0001/q-author-
00008-00000055?rskey=v2pdE7&result=1

p.52 Adapted from *The Oxford Companion to Philosophy* (2nd ed.) by Ted Honderich.
Copyright Oxford University Press 2005. http://www.oxfordreference.
com/view/10.1093/acref/9780199264797.001.0001/acref-9780199264797-e-
2345?rskey=JwDMrk&result=1

p.56 Charles Dana in *Oxford Essential Quotations* (5th ed.) edited by
Susan Ratcliffe. Copyright Oxford University Press 2017. http://www.
oxfordreference.com/view/10.1093/acref/9780191843730.001.0001/q-oro-ed5-
00003427?rskey=E4IG30&result=3

p.59 Adapted from *A Dictionary of Nursing*, (7th ed.), by Elizabeth A. Martin and Tanya
A. McFerran. Copyright Oxford University Press 2017. http://www.oxfordreference.
com/view/10.1093/acref/9780198788454.001.0001/acref-9780198788454-e-
6158?rskey=Gw0d9d&result=1

p.59 Adapted from *A Dictionary of Public Health*, edited by John M. Last. Copyright
Oxford University Press 2007. http://www.oxfordreference.com/view/10.1093/
acref/9780195160901.001.0001/acref-9780195160901-e-3498?rskey=ux2P4p&result=10

p.63 Alan Kay in *Oxford Essential Quotations* (5th ed.) edited by Susan Ratcliffe. Copyright
Oxford University Press 2017. http://www.oxfordreference.com/view/10.1093/
acref/9780191843730.001.0001/q-oro-ed5-00006158?rskey=ny10V5&result=1

p.66 Adapted from *A Dictionary of Sports Studies* by Alan Tomlinson. Copyright
Oxford University Press 2010. http://www.oxfordreference.com/view/10.1093/
acref/9780199213818.001.0001/acref-9780199213818-e-50?rskey=mopauI&result=5

p.70 Michael Eisner in *The Oxford Dictionary of American Quotations* (2nd ed.) edited by
Hugh Rawson and Margaret Miner. Copyright Oxford University Press 2008. http://
www.oxfordreference.com/view/10.1093/acref/9780195168235.001.0001/q-author-
00008-00000506?rskey=SYfqVo&result=1

p.73 T.S. Eliot in *Oxford Essential Quotations* (5th ed.) edited by Susan Ratcliffe. Copyright
Oxford University Press 2017. http://www.oxfordreference.com/view/10.1093/
acref/9780191843730.001.0001/q-oro-ed5-00004036?rskey=KJNVnE&result=1

p.73 Adapted from *The Oxford Companion to the Body* by Colin Blakemore and Sheila
Jennett. Copyright Oxford University Press 2003. http://www.oxfordreference.
com/view/10.1093/acref/9780198524038.001.0001/acref-9780198524038-e-
807?rskey=zBEznQ&result=12

p.77 Andy Rooney in *The Oxford Dictionary of American Quotations* (2nd ed.) edited by Hugh
Rawson and Margaret Miner. Copyright Oxford University Press 2008. http://www.
oxfordreference.com/view/10.1093/acref/9780195168235.001.0001/q-author-00008-
00001393?rskey=oqcSD9&result=1

p.80 adapted from *The Oxford Encyclopedia of the History of American Science, Medicine, and
Technology*, edited by Hugh Richard Slotten. Copyright Oxford university Press 2015.
http://www.oxfordreference.com/view/10.1093/acref/9780199766666.001.0001/acref-
9780199766666-e-439?rskey=mi8pQD&result=2

p.84 John Henry Newman in *Oxford Essential Quotations* (5th ed.) edited
by Susan Ratcliffe. Copyright Oxford University Press 2017. http://www.
oxfordreference.com/view/10.1093/acref/9780191843730.001.0001/q-oro-ed5-
00007827?rskey=0txtiH&result=2

Contents

1 Identity

Have and has ▶1.1

1 Choose the best answer.

1   I *has / have* a lot of friends.
2   We *has / have* classes together.
3   My sister *has / have* a car. She drives to work.
4   Does your roommate *has / have* a job?
5   Your boss *has / have* a nice personality.

2 Correct the incorrect sentences.

1   I have a new roommate!

   _____

2   My roommate have lots of clothes.

   _____

3   She doesn't has a pet.

   _____

4   Do you has a roommate?

   _____

5   Do they has similar personalities?

   _____

6   We have a big kitchen in our apartment.

   _____

The verb *Be* ▶1.2

3 Choose all the answers that correctly complete the sentence.

1   _____ is very serious.

   ☐ They   ☐ We   ☐ She   ☐ My brother

2   _____'s 55.

   ☐ I   ☐ You   ☐ He   ☐ She

3   _____ are co-workers.

   ☐ They   ☐ We   ☐ It   ☐ You

4   _____ isn't my roommate.

   ☐ I   ☐ He   ☐ You   ☐ We

5   _____ aren't in my class.

   ☐ You   ☐ I   ☐ He   ☐ They

4 Use the correct *be* verb and contractions to write positive (+) or negative (–) sentences as indicated.

1   I / a caring person +

   I'm a caring person.

2   She / really funny +

   _____

3   He / 40 –

   _____

4   This class / boring –

   _____

5   We / at the meetup +

   _____

Questions with *be* ▶1.3

5 Match the questions with the correct responses.

~~Who is your roommate?~~   Are you busy?
Is this your apartment?   Are you a student?
What is your schedule?

1   *Who is your roommate?* _____

   June's my roommate.

2   _____

   Yes, it is.

3   _____

   Yes, a little.

4   _____

   It's Monday through Friday 9 to 5.

5   _____

   No, I'm not. I don't go to school.

6 Complete the conversations with the correct form of *be* and pronouns.

1   A: _____Is_____ your apartment clean?

   B: No, _____it's_____ not.

2   A: _____ they friendly?

   B: Yes, _____.

3   A: _____ your friend shy?

   B: No, _____. She's outgoing.

4   A: _____ he a student?

   B: Yes, _____.

Personality adjectives ▶1.1

1 For each pair, write *S* (similar) or *D* (different).

____ 1 calm / quiet   ____ 4 honest / serious

____ 2 shy / fun   ____ 5 friendly / outgoing

____ 3 loud / lazy

2 Match the comments with the phrases in the box.

stay calm	fun to be around	always honest
lazy at times	serious student	sometimes shy

1 "When I'm around new people, I don't like to talk."

_____

2 "On the weekends, I sleep late. I don't like to clean. I don't like to be very busy." _____

3 "I tell people exactly what I think. I don't lie."

_____

4 "I am a happy person. People like me."

_____

5 "I study and read a lot. I like doing homework and working." _____

6 "When I have a lot to do, I don't get upset. I breathe slowly. I count to ten." _____

3 Match the questions in A with the answers in B.

A

1 What do you do to feel calm?   ____

2 What makes someone fun to be around?   ____

3 When do you feel lazy?   ____

4 What are you serious about?   ____

5 When is it very important to be honest? ____

6 How do you know someone is shy?   ____

B

a at night after I finish my work

b the person doesn't talk and is quiet

c my classes and my homework

d at a job interview

e the person is happy and likes to laugh

f listen to music or go for a walk

VOCABULARY DEVELOPMENT: Adverbs of degree ▶1.3

4 Complete the sentences with an adverb of degree. Identify the adjective it tells about.

1 My teacher is **f**___airly___ young. I think she is 25.

2 Takako is **r**_____ fun. She is a great roommate.

3 You keep your apartment really clean. I'm **s**_____ of messy.

4 This is a **p**_____ comfortable sofa. Where did you get it?

5 I like this neighborhood a lot. It's **v**_____ cool.

6 This place is a **b**_____ cheaper than my last apartment. I pay one hundred dollars less.

7 I'm **k**_____ **of** serious. I like to study.

5 Complete the sentences with an adverb of degree from Exercise 4.

Weaker Adverb

1 I'm _____ tired. Can I call you later?

2 I can't hear you. You sound _____ quiet.

3 I'm feeling _____ jealous of you. I want to go.

Adverb in between Weak and Strong

4 I think my room is _____ clean, but my mom probably doesn't think so.

5 It was a _____ good book. You might like it.

Stronger Adverb

6 Wow! This apartment is _____ expensive!

7 Can you turn down your TV? It's _____ loud.

6 Rewrite the sentence using the adverb of degree.

1 My roommate is clean. (fairly)

_____

2 Our apartment is close to school. (pretty)

_____

3 It's an expensive neighborhood. (kind of)

_____

4 The apartment is small. (a little)

_____

READING SKILL: Recognizing descriptions ▶1.1

1 Read the sentences, and find the number of adjectives in parentheses.

1 Mark does not talk a lot or laugh. He studies. He is serious.   (1)
2 Rosa does not like to clean. She is a lazy roommate.   (1)
3 Takako laughs and talks a lot. She is a very outgoing person.   (1)
4 Erik has a nice personality. He is quiet and calm.   (3)
5 Tania listens to music. It is loud. She's a noisy neighbor.   (2)

2 Find the adjectives in **bold** in the reading below. Then complete the sentences with *is* or *is not* to describe each person.

1 Bezhan _____is_____ Anika's **new** roommate.

2 Bezhan _____ **excited**.

3 Bezhan _____ **serious**.

4 Anika _____ **fun**.

5 Anika _____ a **serious** student.

6 Anika _____ **ready**.

READING: Practice

3 Read the emails. Do you think the writers will be friends? Why or why not?

Email between Roommates

Subject: Hi Roommate!

Hi Anika,

My name is Bezhan. I am your new roommate! I'm 18. I'm from Egypt. I'm in the business school. I like to listen to music and dance! I have so many clothes to pack! Are you ready for college?

I'm excited to meet you!

Bezhan

"The greatest thing in the world is to know how to be oneself." —Montaigne

Re: Hi Roommate!

Hi Bezhan,

I love the quote at the end of your email! I'm 19, and I am from India. I'm not ready! I have a lot of books to pack! I love reading. I am a serious student, but I'm fun! ☺

What do you think of this quote? *"The things that we love tell us what we are."* —Thomas Merton

Anika

—Montaigne, selected from *Oxford Essential Quotations*, 5th ed., edited by Susan Ratcliffe
—Thomas Merton, selected from *Oxford Essential Quotations*, 5th ed., edited by Susan Ratcliffe

4 Correct the incorrect sentences.

1 Bezhan likes to dance.

_____

2 Anika has a lot of clothes.

_____

3 Bezhan is in music school.

_____

4 Anika likes reading.

_____

5 Bezhan has a quote at the end of her email from Montaigne.

_____

6 Anika is 20.

_____

5 Answer the questions. Choose *Yes*, *No*, or *Not Given*.

		Yes	No	Not Given
1	Is Anika getting ready for college?	☐	☐	☐
2	Is Bezhan shy?	☐	☐	☐
3	Is Bezhan 18?	☐	☐	☐
4	Is Anika from Egypt?	☐	☐	☐
5	Is Anika outgoing?	☐	☐	☐

6 Complete the sentences with words from the reading.

1 Bezhan's email ends with a quote. It says, "The greatest thing in the world is to know

_____ to be oneself." Bezhan knows herself. She likes _____ and dancing.

2 Anika shares a quote. It says, "The things that we _____ tell us _____ we are."

Anika has a lot of _____. She loves _____. She is a _____ student.

3 Bezhan asks Anika a question. She says, "Are you _____ for college?"

4 Anika answers the question. She says, "I'm _____!"

5 Bezhan and Anika share information about themselves. They are _____ roommates.

They are _____ to meet.

REAL-WORLD ENGLISH: Greeting and introductions ▶1.4

1 Order the dialogue to match the video.

Andy

____ Fine, thanks. How are you? Oh…hey, we have a sociology class together, right?

____ Nice to meet you. I'm Andy.

Sam

____ Yeah! My name's Sam.

____ Hey, how's it going?

____ Hey Sue! She's on the debate team and a future lawyer, too!

2 Look at the picture. Choose the sentences that are acceptable for a professor to say in this situation.

1 Good morning, everyone.   ____

2 Hello. How do you do?   ____

3 I'm Tamara Bertelli. Welcome.   ____

4 Hey! How are ya?   ____

5 Nice to meet you all.   ____

6 You're late! Ha! It's just a joke. ____

3 Correct the expressions that are not acceptable to say when meeting the friend of a friend.

1 Hello, you must be…

_____

2 What's up?

_____

3 Hi! My name's…

_____

4 Nice to meet you. I'm…

_____

5 How do you do?

_____

6 Good morning, all.

_____

LISTENING SKILL: Understanding affirmative and negative contractions ▶1.3

1 🔊 Listen to the sentences. Are the contractions in the sentences correct? Write *Yes* or *No*.

1   Hi, we're back with Sheila Gurney.   _____

2   Sheila, you're a manager.   _____

3   It isn't interesting.   _____

4   Well…they're the same.   _____

5   They aren't very serious.   _____

UNIT REVIEW: Podcast

🔊 **GO ONLINE to listen to the podcast from the Unit Review.**

2 🔊 Listen to the Unit Review Podcast. Complete the sentences with words from the podcast.

1   You interview people and decide who gets the _____.

2   It's really _____ to find information online.

3   They use social media for work and to post information about their school and _____ history.

4   In photos, people have _____.

5   The person online and the person in the _____ don't match.

3 🔊 Listen again. Which sentences does Shelia agree with?

1   It's good for managers to look at a person's online profile.   ☐

2   People post boring photos.   ☐

3   Do not post all your photos online.   ☐

4   People are the same online and at work.   ☐

5   Smart people post only a little information online.   ☐

DISCUSSION BOARD PREPARATION

4 Look at the Unit 1 Review Discussion Point. Read the questions in the prompt. Then read the reply. Label the part of the reply that answers question 1 from the prompt. Then label the part that answers question 2.

5 Does the student agree or disagree with the quote from Mark Zuckerberg? Label the sentences that best show the writer's opinion.

6 What words and examples does the writer use to describe the two identities?

At school _____

With friends _____

7 Look at the last two sentences of the reply. What is the purpose of these sentences? What do they tell you?

_____

Unit 1 Review Discussion Point

1 Read the quote. Do you have one identity at school or work? Is it different from your identity with friends and family?
   "You have one identity...The days of you having a different image for your work friends or co-workers and for the other people you know are probably coming to an end pretty quickly."
   —Mark Zuckerberg, from *Oxford Essential Quotations*, 5th ed., edited by Susan Ratcliffe

2 What parts of your identity are the same when you are with different people? What parts change?

Latest: Yuan Li
one hour ago
I have a different identity at school. At school, I'm shy. I don't like to answer questions. I don't use a loud voice. I listen. But I'm different with my friends. They say I'm funny. I love to talk, and I like to laugh. I am loud!
    Some parts of my identity are the same with different people. Most people think I'm fun to be around. Many friends don't know I'm kind of serious. I am a little bit serious, but not with new friends. A person has to know me for a long time. Then they see all my different identities.

8 Overall, did the writer answer all the questions? If yes, explain. If no, what can the writer change?

_____

_____

9 Review the rubric. Use the rubric to give a score for the reply.
Give points: 0 (not successful)–10 (successful).

Writing a Discussion Board Post	Points
The post answers the questions clearly and completely.	
The post has an opening sentence and a closing sentence.	
The post shows careful thinking about the topic.	
The post uses adjectives to describe and gives examples.	
The verbs *be* and *has/have* are used correctly.	
The post is long enough (100–150 words).	
Total	

WRITE YOUR POST

10 Read the quote. Do you have one identity at school or work? Is it different from your identity with friends and family? Write a draft of your post for the Unit 1 Review Discussion Point.

"You have one identity...The days of you having a different image for your work friends or co-workers and for the other people you know are probably coming to an end pretty quickly."
—Mark Zuckerberg, from *Oxford Essential Quotations*, 5th ed., edited by Susan Ratcliffe

11 Use the rubric from Exercise 9 to score your post. Then improve your post.

Go online to add your comments to the discussion board.

2 Relationships

Possessive adjectives ▶2.1

1 Use the correct possessive adjective to complete each sentence.

1 I have a new colleague. _____ name is Maria.
   Her / Our / My

2 Hi Ben! How are you? I can't wait to meet _____ family! *his / their / your*

3 I have two nephews. _____ names are Ali and Kamil. *His / Their / Our*

4 My family has dinner every night together. We talk about _____ day. *your / our / their*

2 Complete the conversations with possessive adjectives.

1 A: Excuse me, is that _____ laptop?
   B: No, _____ laptop is right here next to me.

2 A: David's parents have a new car, right? Is that _____ car?
   B: No, that isn't it. _____ new car is red.

3 A: Is Sue on _____ phone?
   B: No, she has Max's phone. I don't know why she is using _____ phone.

4 A: Does your grandfather live with you in _____ house?
   B: Yes, we take care of him in _____ house.

Nouns: Countable, uncountable, and plural ▶2.2

3 Choose *SC* (singular countable), *PC* (plural countable), or *U* (uncountable).

	SC	PC	U
1 too much information	☐	☐	☐
2 my niece	☐	☐	☐
3 some time	☐	☐	☐
4 our families	☐	☐	☐

4 Read the conversation and find five uncountable nouns.

A: How do you like your new apartment?
B: It's great! I get a lot of light on the third floor.
A: Nice! And how about your roommate, Daria?
B: We get coffee together every morning! She's really nice, and she knows a lot about the city. She has good information on restaurants and things to do.
A: That sounds great!
B: Yeah, it is. She's smart and interesting, but she is also messy. She leaves a lot of stuff all over the apartment.
A: Well, no one is perfect.
B: Yeah, that's true. I'm kind of messy too, I guess. Oh well! We have a lot of fun together. I'm excited for this year!

Possessive 's and possessive pronouns ▶2.3

5 Write the apostrophes in the correct place.

1 These are Amals brothers, Khalid and Ibrihim.
2 I'm going to Victorias apartment on the first floor.
3 That is Bens niece, not his sister.
4 My colleagues name is June Lee.
5 Toms cousins are Anatolie and Jeramiah.
6 In ten minutes, I have to go to my grandparents house.

6 Rewrite the sentences to use possessive pronouns.

1 That is my nephew's bike.
   That is his.

2 Is that her backpack?
   _____

3 His game is on Saturday. My game is on Sunday.
   _____

4 Our house is next to their house.
   _____

5 I have my phone. Where is your phone?
   _____

6 Your apartment is not close. Do you want to come to our apartment? It's closer.
   _____

Family ▶2.2

1 Unscramble the family words to complete the sentences.

1 My brother has daughters, so I have

   I C N E E S.   _____

2 In the family picture, there are eight

   G C A N I L H R D N E D R.   _____

3 My best friend does not have children, but she has

   four E W N E H S P.   _____

4 I don't live with my parents. I live in Mexico City with

   my R P E N G T R A D A N S.   _____

5 My best friend is also my

   O C U S I N.   _____

2 Write the opposite of the **bold** word.

1 My **uncle** lives in Cuba.   _____

2 My **niece** is eight years old.   _____

3 I **don't stay with** my little brother

   when my mom is at work.   _____

4 I have four **grandchildren**.   _____

5 My **aunt** lives with us.   _____

3 Choose the correct words to complete the paragraph.

I have a very big family. My mom has three brothers.
My ¹*uncles / aunts* are a lot of fun. They play games with
us. They are all married. My mom also has one sister, so
there are four ²*aunts / nieces* in my family. My uncles and
aunts have kids, so my mom has three ³*nieces / aunts* and
four ⁴*nephews / grandchildren*. We like to get together
with my ⁵*grandparents / grandchildren* at their house.

VOCABULARY DEVELOPMENT: Verb + preposition ▶2.3

4 Match the beginning of the sentence in A with the ending in B.

A

1 I read a book while I wait   ____

2 Mara likes to spend time   ____

3 With my friend at work, I talk   ____

4 I am really busy. I have to work   ____

B

a about our boss and our busy schedule.

b for the bus.

c with her little sister after school.

d on a presentation.

5 Match a verb in A to a presposition in B and complete the sentences below. Use the correct verb form.

A

agree	talk	work	write

B

about	on	to	with

1 My friend _____ her life with her new

   baby a lot. It is hard to take care of a baby!

2 When I _____ someone important,

   I ask a friend to read the email to make sure it's OK.

3 At my school, we _____ homework by

   ourselves. We have to complete it on our own.

4 My sister and I always _____ each other.

   We have similar feelings about almost everything.

6 Correct the mistakes in verb + preposition.

1 I agree on my parents. My brother needs to get a job.

   _____*agree with*_____

2 People don't write letters of friends anymore.

   They use email. _____

3 My grandparents ask to my help with paying their

   bills online. _____

4 My friend says she really needs to talk of me tonight!

   _____

REAL-WORLD READING

READING: Practice

1 Read the text. What sentences have the most important ideas?

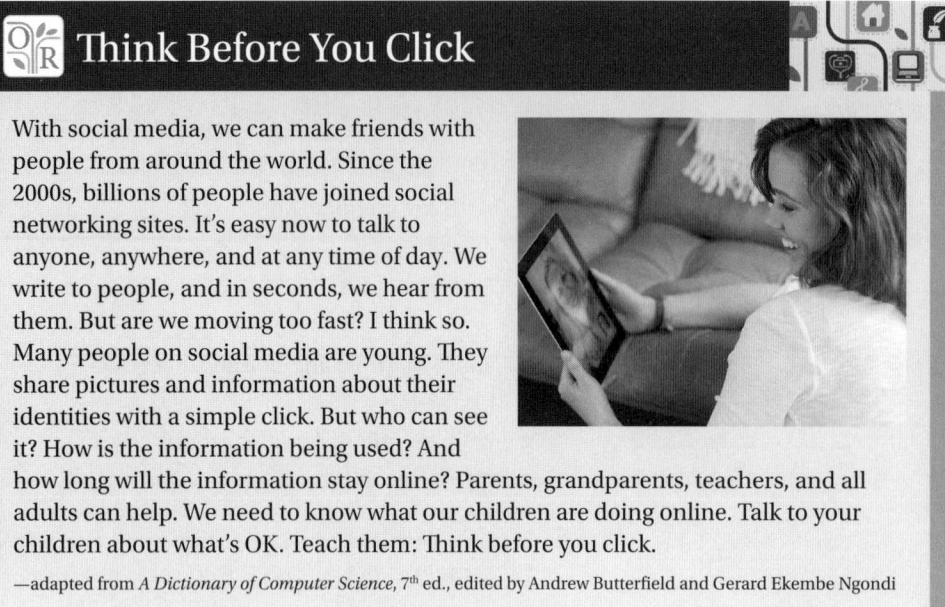

Think Before You Click

With social media, we can make friends with people from around the world. Since the 2000s, billions of people have joined social networking sites. It's easy now to talk to anyone, anywhere, and at any time of day. We write to people, and in seconds, we hear from them. But are we moving too fast? I think so. Many people on social media are young. They share pictures and information about their identities with a simple click. But who can see it? How is the information being used? And how long will the information stay online? Parents, grandparents, teachers, and all adults can help. We need to know what our children are doing online. Talk to your children about what's OK. Teach them: Think before you click.

—adapted from *A Dictionary of Computer Science*, 7th ed., edited by Andrew Butterfield and Gerard Ekembe Ngondi

2 Read the text. Then correct the mistakes in the sentences.

1 Since the 2000s, millions of people have joined these sites.

   Since the 2000s, billions of people have joined these sites.

2 We write to people, and in minutes, we hear from them.

3 Many people on social media are adults.

4 Parents, grandparents, managers, and all adults can help.

5 We need to know what our parents are doing online.

3 Read the sentences. Choose *True*, *False*, or *Not Given*.

	True	False	Not Given
1 Social media helps us make friends.	☐	☐	☐
2 People share credit card information online a lot.	☐	☐	☐
3 Many young people have email accounts.	☐	☐	☐
4 It's not easy to share information online.	☐	☐	☐
5 People should always share information about their identity.	☐	☐	☐

4 Use the words and phrases in the box to replace the **bold** words.

be available	enter information online	children
post content	the Internet	

1 Think before you **click**. _____

2 **Social media** allows us to make friends anywhere. _____

3 Many people on social media are **young**. _____

4 They **share pictures and information** about their identities with a simple click.

_____

5 How long will the information **stay online?** _____

READING SKILL: Identifying audience and purpose ▶2.2

5 Choose the correct answers.

1 This text is from _____.

   a an email   b a newspaper

2 The author uses the pronouns _____, so people think like her.

   a *we* and *our*   b *you* and *your*

3 The writer's purpose is to _____.

   a explain social media with facts and examples   b change what people do online

4 The author shares _____.

   a facts and opinions   b stories and information about her identity

5 The author uses _____ to get the audience to think.

   a questions   b facts

6 Read each sentence. Is the purpose to share a fact or get the audience to think? Choose *Fact* or *Think*. One sentence has both Fact and Think answers.

	Fact	Think
1 Since the 2000s, billions of people have joined social networking sites and are now friends.	☐	☐
2 Many people on social media are young.	☐	☐
3 They share pictures and information about their identities with a simple click.	☐	☐
4 How is the information being used?	☐	☐
5 How long will the information stay online?	☐	☐

REAL-WORLD ENGLISH: Asking someone to repeat something ▶2.4

1 🔍 Watch the video and match the statements to the responses.

____ 1   Sorry, Kevin…I didn't catch that.

____ 2   Sorry, did you say you're from the UK?

____ 3   Sorry. Say that again.

____ 4   Wait, I didn't catch that. You were what?

a   Chuffed. Very happy.

b   Yeah, yeah. That's right. So I stayed here and worked on some art projects. I sold a few paintings, actually.

c   I sold some paintings.

d   Oh. I said, 'What did you do this summer?'

2 Choose the correct words to complete the sentences.

Conversation 1

A: Hey, Ann. I'm sorry I'm running a little late. I'll be there in 15 minutes.

B: Did you *say / repeat* 50 minutes?

A: No, 15. I said I'll see you in 15 minutes.

Conversation 2

A: Hi, I have an appointment at 10. I'm Ben Zimmerson.

B: Could you *please / sorry* repeat that.

A: Yeah, last name Zimmerson, first name Ben. I have an appointment at 10.

Conversation 3

A: Hi, I'm Shelia's sister, Zadie.

B: I'm sorry, I didn't *hear / say* that.

A: I'm Zadie. Shelia is my sister.

B: Oh yeah, nice to meet you, Zadie. Shelia says you're here for the weekend?

A: Yeah! I'm excited. We are going to my aunt's art show.

B: *What / That*?

A: My aunt is a painter, and she has a show this weekend.

3 Order the dialogue.

Office Assistant

____   I'm sorry. What time did you say?

____   Oh, OK. Do you have an appointment?

____   Well, you're a little early. Why don't you have a seat? I'm sure she'll be back soon.

Student with Appointment

____   I said 1:30 this afternoon?

_1_   Hi, I'm here to see Professor Dickerson.

____   Yeah, for 1:30.

____   Alright, thanks.

____   I'm sorry, Professor, I didn't hear that.

Professor

____   Oh, hi Yuan! I'll be with you in a moment.

____   I said I just need a minute and then we can meet. Thanks for waiting.

LISTENING SKILL: Recognizing the end of a sentence ▶2.1

1 🔊 Listen. Rewrite the sentences into the two sentences you hear.

1 We want to hear from you what problems do you have?

_____

2 And we've got a call yes, hello?

_____

3 They have so much to do I want them to have free time.

_____

4 And also ask her to spend some time with you too you'll feel closer.

_____

UNIT REVIEW: Podcast

🔊 **Go online to listen to the podcast from the Unit Review.**

2 🔊 Listen to the Unit Review Podcast, and choose the sentence you hear.

1 ___ a We are talking about family relationships.
___ b We are talking about work relationships.

2 ___ a I take care of my children after school.
___ b I take care of my grandchildren after school.

3 ___ a I don't always agree with their parents.
___ b I don't always agree with their grandparents.

3 🔊 Listen to the Unit Review Podcast. Write *T* (True) or *F* (False).

___ 1 The purpose of the show is to give advice.

___ 2 The caller agrees with her family member.

___ 3 The caller wants her daughter to have free time.

___ 4 The host agrees with the caller.

DISCUSSION BOARD PREPARATION

4 Look at the Unit 2 Review Discussion Point. Read the questions in the prompt. Then read the reply. Label the part of the reply that answers question 1 from the prompt. Then label the parts that answer question 2.

5 Does the student agree with the quote? Why or why not?

_____

6 Do you think the radio host from the Unit Podcast agrees with the student? Why or why not?

_____

Unit 2 Review Discussion Point

1   Read the quote. Do you agree? Why or why not?
     "To like and dislike the same things, that is indeed true friendship."
     —Sallust (86–35 BC), Roman historian, from *Oxford Essential Quotations*, 4ᵗʰ ed.
2   Give two examples to support your opinion.

Latest: **Liam Borelli**
one hour ago
Yes, I agree with this quote. The first thing you talk about with new people is things you like. It's like a game. You find out the things that you both like. Then you have a lot to talk about. Then you become friends.
   For example, my roommate and I speak different languages. We are from different cultures, but we like the same movies. We can talk for hours about movies and also sports. Now my roommate is my close friend.
   Another example is on social media. I find so many friends because we like the same music, TV shows, and other things. We are like a family. We talk so much every day.

7 Overall, did the writer answer all the questions? If yes, explain. If no, what can the writer change?

_____

_____

8 Review the rubric. Use the rubric to give a score for the reply.
Give points: 0 (not successful)–10 (successful).

Writing a Discussion Board Post	Points
The writer explains why he or she agrees/disagrees with the quote.	
The post has an opening sentence and a closing sentence.	
The post has two examples.	
The writer uses countable and uncountable nouns and plurals correctly.	
The writer uses possessive adjectives, possessive 's, and possessive pronouns correctly.	
The post is long enough (100–150 words).	
Total	

WRITE YOUR POST

9 Read the quote. Do you agree? Why or why not? Write a draft of your post for the Unit 2 Review Discussion Point.

     "To like and dislike the same things, that is indeed true friendship."
     —Sallust (86–35 BC), Roman historian, from *Oxford Essential Quotations*, 4ᵗʰ ed.,
     edited by Susan Ratcliffe

10 Use the rubric from Exercise 8 to score your post. Then improve your post.

Go online to add your comments to the discussion board.

3 Responsibilities

Simple present: Positive, negative, and *yes/no* questions ▶3.1

1 Choose the correct question.

1 A: *Do you go grocery shopping?*
     Does you go grocery shopping?
   B: Yes, I do. I go on Saturdays.
2 A: *Does your roommate like to clean?*
     Do your roommate like to clean?
   B: No, he doesn't.
3 A: *Does your friends study English?*
     Do your friends study English?
   B: Yes, they study English.
4 A: *Does most people volunteer?*
     Do most people volunteer?
   B: Yes, most people volunteer.

2 Complete the conversations using the simple present.

1 A: ___Do___ you like to fold clothes?
   B: Yes, ___I do___.
2 A: _____ your roommate prepare meals at home?
   B: Yes, _____.
3 A: _____ most people wash dishes by hand?
   B: No, _____.
4 A: _____ most people pay bills online?
   B: Yes, _____.

The simple present and adverbs of frequency ▶3.2

3 Are the sentences correct? Choose *Yes* or *No*.

		Yes	No
1	She washes always the dishes.	☐	☐
2	I don't never cut the grass.	☐	☐
3	Usually, we change the sheets.	☐	☐
4	You hardly ever fold the clothes.	☐	☐
5	I clean the often carpets.	☐	☐

4 Match an adverb in A to a verb in B and complete the sentences. Use the correct verb form.

A

always	often	usually	hardly ever

B

cut	fold	go	pay

1 I don't _____ laundry. Often, my husband does it.
2 My roommate _____ grocery shopping. She enjoys looking for new foods.
3 My friend _____ her bills on time. She is never late.
4 They _____ the grass. It's really long.

Subject and object questions in the simple present ▶3.3

5 Complete the sentences with *do*, *does*, or – (nothing).

1 What housework _____ you do?
2 Who _____ has the most responsibilities?
3 What subjects _____ your friend like?
4 Where _____ is your job?
5 What kind of job _____ you want?

6 Make subject and object questions in the simple present. Then answer the questions about you.

1 languages / you / speak / what /do /
   What languages do you speak_____?
   I speak Amharic, Arabic, and English_____.
2 close friend / is / who / your
   _____?
   _____.
3 kind of work / fun / is / what
   _____?
   _____.
4 responsibilities / you / what / do / have
   _____?
   _____.

Unit 3   Responsibilities   15

Household chores ▶3.1

1 Match each verb with a noun from the box.

bills	carpets	clothes	dishes	garbage	meals

1 pay   _____

2 prepare   _____

3 fold   _____

4 empty the   _____

5 clean the   _____

6 wash the   _____

2 Read the text. Complete the paragraph with a phrase from the box.

cut the grass	clean the carpets
go grocery shopping	prepare a meal

What chores do people like?

Here are the chores in order from one to four. Most

people like to ¹_____. It's fun to shop for

food. Next on the list is ²_____. People

usually enjoy cooking. Number three on the list is

³_____. People like to be outside, but

they don't enjoy working so hard. Number four is

⁴_____. Most people think cleaning the

floor is boring.

VOCABULARY DEVELOPMENT:
Time expressions ▶3.2

3 Write the words in the correct order to make sentences.

1 volunteer / once / I / month / a

_____

2 cleans / the / on / Jonah / carpets / Sundays

_____

3 looks at / several / a day / social media / He / times

_____

4 Shelia / a while / her neighbors / once / talks to / in

_____

5 watch / every / My parents / the news / day

_____

4 Read the chart, and complete the sentences with a time expression.

	Teri	Peter
watches the news	M, T, W, Th, F	1/week
talks to neighbors	1/day	2/month
visits a local park	Saturdays	Not often

1 Teri watches the news ___every weekday___.

2 Peter watches the news _____.

3 Teri talks to neighbors _____.

4 Peter talks to neighbors _____.

5 Teri visits a local park _____.

6 Peter does not visit a local park _____.

Work-related words ▶3.3

5 Choose the correct answers.

1 I don't think I have the _____ the

company wants. I am a sales associate, not a manager.

a programs   b work exprience

2 I manage people and schedules. I have a lot of

_____.

a responsibilities   b customers

3 I work with computers. I _____

software programs.

a serve   b develop

4 In the lab, we do _____.

a research   b decisions

6 Use the phrases in the box to replace the **bold** words.

decisions	develop	projects	serve

1 How many customers do you **help** each day?

_____

2 I **create** apps. _____

3 I make **judgments** about who to hire.

_____

4 At school. I work on lots of different **assignments**.

_____

     Unit 3   Responsibilities

READING SKILL: Recognizing and understanding contrast linking words:
But and *however* ▶ 3.1

1 Match the contrasting ideas.

1 I wash the dishes every day. _____ a You fold them once a month.

2 You have a busy schedule. _____ b You hardly ever cut it.

3 I cut the grass several times a month. _____ c You only wash them once in a while.

4 I fold clean clothes once a week. _____ d You only prepare them on Sundays.

5 I always prepare the meals on weekdays. _____ e You aren't the only busy person I know.

2 Complete the sentences with *but* or *however*. Put commas in the correct places. Then find the sentences in the text.

1 We go to work, and we get money for it. _____ what about the work at home?

2 These chores usually take a lot of time _____ there's no pay.

3 One person does chores every day _____ the other works at home once in a while.

4 One answer is to pay other people to do the work. _____ not everyone has the money.

5 There is work to do _____ they share the responsibilities.

READING: Practice

3 Read the text. Which paragraph states the problem, and which paragraph gives answers?

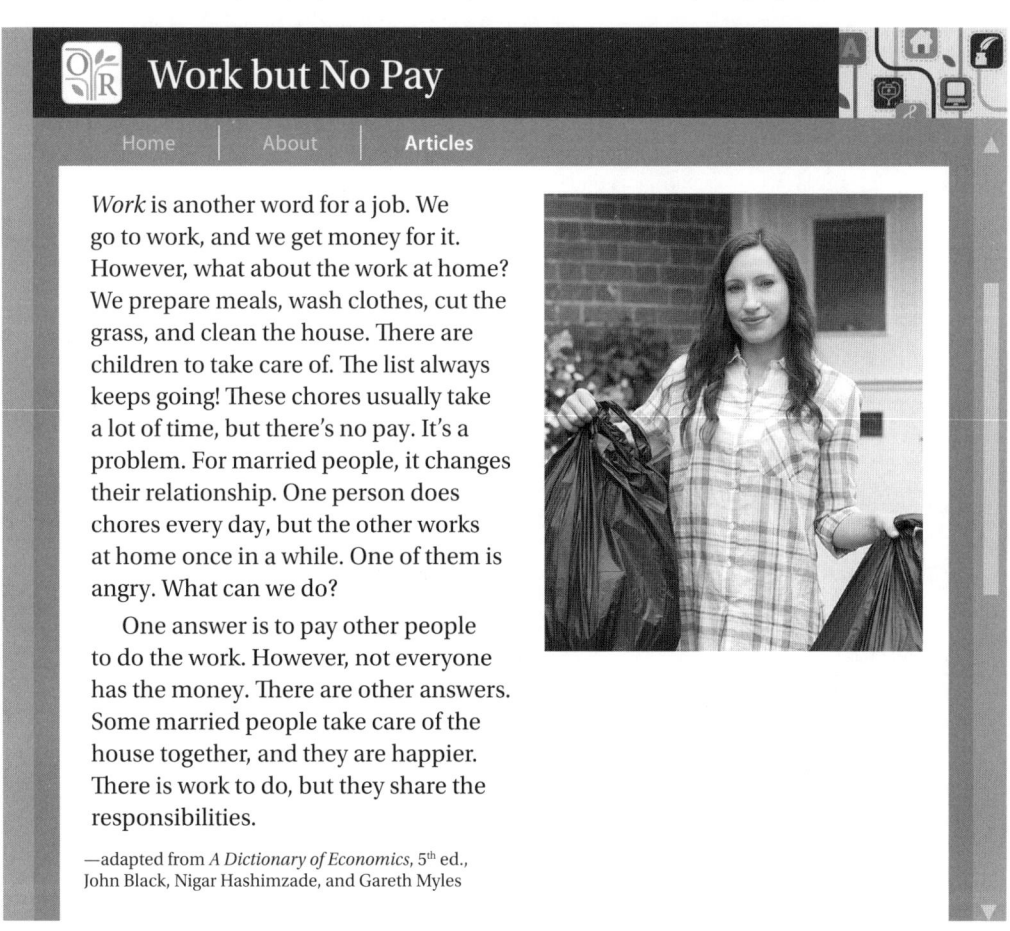

Work but No Pay

| Home | About | **Articles** |

Work is another word for a job. We go to work, and we get money for it. However, what about the work at home? We prepare meals, wash clothes, cut the grass, and clean the house. There are children to take care of. The list always keeps going! These chores usually take a lot of time, but there's no pay. It's a problem. For married people, it changes their relationship. One person does chores every day, but the other works at home once in a while. One of them is angry. What can we do?

One answer is to pay other people to do the work. However, not everyone has the money. There are other answers. Some married people take care of the house together, and they are happier. There is work to do, but they share the responsibilities.

—adapted from *A Dictionary of Economics*, 5th ed., John Black, Nigar Hashimzade, and Gareth Myles

4 Choose the best answer.

1 We *do / do not* get money for the work at home.
2 There are *children / bills* to take care of.
3 For married people, housework *does / does not* change their relationship.
4 Some people pay *children / other people* to take care of the house.
5 Happier people work *together / alone* on the house.

5 Find the words in the text. Then for each pair, write *S* (similar) or *D* (different).

_____ 1 work / job

_____ 2 share the repsonsibilities / one person does the chores

_____ 3 problem / answers

_____ 4 pay / money

_____ 5 clean the house / take care of the house

6 Choose the correct answers.

1 What is an example of a chore from the reading?
   a prepare meals
   b pay other people
   c pay the bills
2 What does "the list always keeps going" mean?
   a there are lots of chores
   b there are many things to write
   c there is no pay
3 Why is someone angry?
   a there is no pay
   b one person is happier
   c one person does more work
4 What is one answer to the problem?
   a one person does all the work
   b pay someone to do the work
   c pay both people to do the work
5 Why are some people happier?
   a one person does more work
   b we can pay people to do the work
   c they share the responsibilities

Unit 3 Responsibilities

REAL-WORLD ENGLISH: Requesting by phone ▶3.4

1 @ Watch the video. Who says these things? Is the statement a direct, a less direct request, or an accepted request?

	Person	Statement
1 I'd like to meet with you.	Max	direct request
2 Sure. What would you like to discuss?		
3 Is it possible to make an appointment for tomorrow after class?		
4 Could I ask you for a favor?		
5 Yeah, I'm watching a movie.		

2 Read the conversation and answer the questions.

Student: Hi, Professor Williams. I'm sorry to bother you. This is James Pierson. I'm in your Tuesday/Thursday Chemistry class.

Professor: Hi, James. It's not a bother. How can I help you?

Student: Well, I'm wondering if it's possible to hand in my project a week late.

Professor: I'm sorry, James, but late assignments aren't accepted. Part of being successful in school is planning your time appropriately to get the work done.

1   The student *uses / does not use* polite language to make his request.
2   The student asks for more *time / help* with his project.
3   The professor *accepts / rejects* the student's request.
4   The professor *is / is not* bothered by the phone call.
5   The student *is / is not* confident the professor will accept his request.

3 Choose the best request for the situation.

1 ____ a   Could you tell me what the homework from class is?

   ____ b   Could I ask a huge favor? Can I get the homework from class?

2 ____ a   I'd like to use your apartment for a study session. Mine is too small.

   ____ b   Can I ask you a big favor? Could I use your apartment for a study session? Mine is too small.

3 ____ a   Do you have time to help me with calculus? I'm not doing so well in class.

   ____ b   I'd like you to help me with my Calculus class. I'm not doing so well this semester.

4 ____ a   I'd like to practice my presentation. It's an hour long. Can you come over and listen?

   ____ b   Sorry to bother you, but I'd like to practice my presentation. It's an hour long. Do you have time to listen?

5 ____ a   I'm wondering if it is possible for you to give me a ride downtown. I know you're studying for a test, but I'm running late for my interview.

   ____ b   Could I get a ride downtown? I know you're studying for a test, but I'm running late for my interview.

LISTENING SKILL: Recognizing linkers for addition ▶3.3

1 🔊 Listen. Write the linker for addition you hear in the sentence.

1 _____   4 _____

2 _____   5 _____

3 _____

UNIT REVIEW: Podcast

Go online to listen to the podcast from the Unit Review.

2 🔊 Listen to the Unit Review Podcast. Choose the correct answer.

1   What people does the charity serve?
   a   people new to the country   b   people working in the community

2   What classes do they have?
   a   English and computer classes   b   job skills and English classes

3   What is a responsibility Mr. Ruskin has?
   a   make decisions about the programs   b   teach English

4   What is one thing that happens if they don't get the money?
   a   people don't get jobs   b   people don't get money

5   What was Mr. Ruskin 30 years ago?
   a   a community leader   b   new to this country

3 🔊 Listen again, and complete the sentences.

1   We have classes for English _____ a second language.

2   I _____ the organization.

3   I also am _____ for getting money for our charity work.

4   I am very _____ about my responsibilities.

5   They need you to see the person they _____ become.

DISCUSSION BOARD PREPARATION

4 Look at the Unit 3 Review Discussion Point. Read the questions in the prompt. Then read the reply. Label the part of the reply that answers question 1 from the prompt.

5 What two examples does the student use to support her opinion? What power do they have?

_____

_____

6 What responsibilities does the writer list for the examples?

_____

7 What do the student's examples and the person from the Unit Podcast all have?

_____

Unit 3 Review Discussion Point

1   Read the quote. Why do people with power have more responsibility?
    "Where there's great power, there must also be great responsibility."
    —Lyndon B. Johnson, selected from *The Oxford Dictionary of American Quotations*, 2ⁿᵈ ed., edited by Hugh Rawson and Margaret Miner
2   Give two examples of people in positions of power and describe the responsibilities they have.

> Latest: Maria Turchek
> one hour ago
> People with power have more responsibility. One example is a famous person. We watch famous people on TV and in movies, but we also watch them in their real lives. We want to know everything about them. In addition, children want to be like famous people, so famous people need to be good examples. They have the responsibility to be good. Another example is the manager of a business. This person leads all the workers. When the manager is good, then other people are good but if the manager is not good, then others are not good. Because the manager has the power to make the business a good place for everyone, this is also the manager's responsibility.

---

8 Overall, did the writer answer all the questions? If yes, explain. If no, what can the writer change?

_____

_____

9 Review the rubric. Use the rubric to give a score for the reply.
Give points: 0 (not successful)–10 (successful).

Writing a Discussion Board Post	Points
The post answers the questions clearly and completely.	
The post has two examples of people in power.	
The writer lists the responsibilities the people have.	
The writer uses linking words for contrasts correctly.	
The writer uses linking words for additions correctly.	
The post is long enough (100–150 words).	
Total	

WRITE YOUR POST

10 Read the quote. What does it mean? Write a quote that describes you. Why does this quote describe you? Write your post for the discussion board.

"Where there's great power, there must also be great responsibility."
—Lyndon B. Johnson, selected from *The Oxford Dictionary of American Quotations*, 2ⁿᵈ ed., edited by Hugh Rawson and Margaret Miner

11 Use the rubric from Exercise 9 to score your post. Then improve your post.

  Go online to add your comments to the discussion board.

4 Extremes

How much / How many with countable and uncountable nouns ▶4.1

1 Complete the sentences with *How much* or *How many*.

1 _____ hours of TV do you watch each day?

2 _____ time do you spend on homework each day?

3 _____ pizza do you eat in one week?

4 _____ pieces of cake do you have at one time?

5 _____ meals do you make at home?

6 _____ money do you spend on coffee?

2 Write questions about the **bold** words in the answers. Use *how much* or *how many*.

1 A: _____?

 B: I put a lot of **sugar** in my coffee.

2 A: _____?

 B: I drink five glasses of **water** every day.

3 A: _____?

 B: I work for ten **hours** each day.

4 A: _____?

 B: I have three **brothers**.

5 A: _____?

 B: I run for 80 **minutes** each week.

6 A: _____?

 B: I like a lot of **spice** in my food.

Quantifiers: *a few / a little / a lot / lots* ▶4.2

3 Complete the sentences with the correct quantifier.

a small number/amount

1 She puts _____ of milk in her tea.

2 He has _____ of friends from China.

3 Can I have _____ of more time?

4 I have _____ of things to do this morning.

A big number/amount

5 I eat _____ of pizza every week.

6 There are _____ of fish in this tank.

7 I like _____ of types of food.

4 Write the words in the correct order to make sentences.

1 has / a / money / lot / he / of

 _____

2 few / Daniel / a / knows / people / from Japan

 _____

3 little / a / he / drinks / coffee

 _____

4 lots / energy / she / of / has

 _____

5 grow / few / we / a / vegetables

 _____

There is… / There are… ▶4.3

5 Choose the best answer.

1 There *is / are* a chair next to the table.

2 There *is / are* flowers on top of the table.

3 There *is / are* a light over the table.

4 There *is / are* a rug in front of the table.

5 There *is / are* toys behind the couch.

6 Complete the conversations with the correct form of *there is* or *there are*.

1 A: Is there a bathroom here?

 B: Yes, _____ two bathrooms on the first floor.

2 A: Are there any windows?

 B: Yes, _____ a window over there.

3 A: Is there a swimming pool?

 B: No, _____.

4 A: Are there lots of people here?

 B: No, _____ only two people in this huge house.

5 A: Are there four bedrooms?

 B: No, _____ six.

Describing foods ▶4.1

1 Unscramble the letters and write the words.

1 ypalcti _____ 4 ecfpetr _____

2 eyegnr _____ 5 okoc _____

3 ozfenr _____

2 Use a word from Exercise 1.

1 On a _____ day, I usually have coffee and toast for breakfast.

2 I don't buy _____ foods. I don't have a microwave to heat them up.

3 When I need a lot of _____, I have a cup of coffee and a snack, like nuts.

4 I like to _____ meals at home. It saves money, and I enjoy making them.

5 The cake looks beautiful, and it tastes as good as it looks! It is _____!

3 Match the photo with the description.

___ 1 I love to **cook**. I make a lot of meals at home.

___ 2 On a **typical** day, many people drink this with a little milk or sugar.

___ 3 This is a delicious and **sweet** breakfast. It tastes good with butter and syrup.

___ 4 Eat this **perfect** meal to stay healthy and give you **energy**!

VOCABULARY DEVELOPMENT:
Prepositions of place ▶4.2

4 Complete the sentences with a word or phrase from the box.

behind	beside	in front of	under	over

1 The boat goes _____ the bridge.

2 Cars travel on the bridge _____ water.

3 At lunch, I sit _____ my friends at a table in the café.

4 I don't see the presenter. Someone tall is _____ me.

5 I'm short, so the people _____ me don't have a problem seeing the presenter.

5 For each pair, write *S* (similar) or *D* (different).

___ 1 behind / in front of

___ 2 beside / next to

___ 3 on top of / over

___ 4 under / over

___ 5 in front of / next to

6 Look at the photo. Complete the sentences with words from the box.

behind	on top of	next to	in front of

1 There is a man holding a puppet. The puppet is _____ him.

2 The puppet has a hat _____ its head.

3 There are many puppets hanging _____ and _____ the man.

1 Read the text. Find one typical thing and one not typical thing.

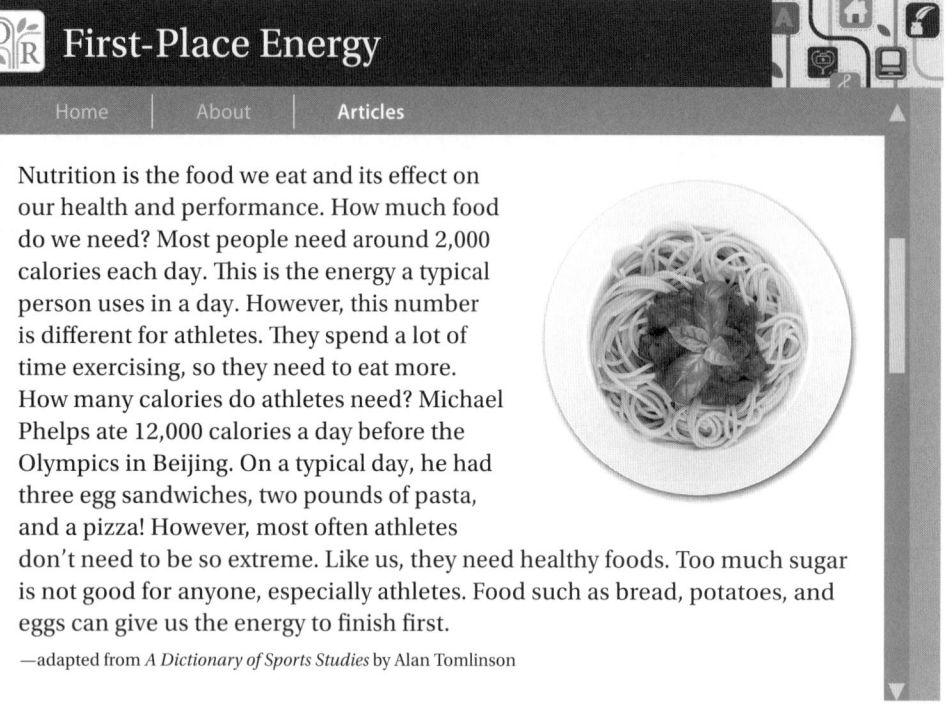

First-Place Energy

| Home | About | **Articles** |

Nutrition is the food we eat and its effect on our health and performance. How much food do we need? Most people need around 2,000 calories each day. This is the energy a typical person uses in a day. However, this number is different for athletes. They spend a lot of time exercising, so they need to eat more. How many calories do athletes need? Michael Phelps ate 12,000 calories a day before the Olympics in Beijing. On a typical day, he had three egg sandwiches, two pounds of pasta, and a pizza! However, most often athletes don't need to be so extreme. Like us, they need healthy foods. Too much sugar is not good for anyone, especially athletes. Food such as bread, potatoes, and eggs can give us the energy to finish first.

—adapted from *A Dictionary of Sports Studies* by Alan Tomlinson

2 Choose the best answer.

1 What is nutrition?
  a the food we eat and its effect on our health
  b our performance and its effect on our health
2 How many calories do typical people need each day?
  a 2,000 calories
  b 12,000 calories
3 Why do athletes need more food?
  a they exercise
  b they enjoy it
4 Which food did Michael Phelps not eat on a typical day?
  a pizza
  b potatoes
5 What is important for athletes?
  a extreme kinds of food
  b healthy kinds of food

3 Choose *True, False,* or *Not Given.*

	True	False	Not Given
1 Most people eat too many calories.	☐	☐	☐
2 Sugar is the perfect food for an athlete.	☐	☐	☐
3 Athletes at the Beijing Olympics ate 12,000 calories a day.	☐	☐	☐
4 Extreme exercise uses a lot of energy.	☐	☐	☐
5 Too much pizza is not good for athletes.	☐	☐	☐

REAL-WORLD READING

4 Write the correct answer.

an athlete	a typical person	pasta
pounds	eggs	sugar

1 Michael Phelps is _____.

2 _____ needs 2,000 calories a day.

3 It is not good to eat too much _____.

4 Michael Phelps ate two _____ of _____.

5 A good food for athletes is _____.

READING SKILL: Recognizing parts of speech, and using them to figure out meaning from context ▶4.1

5 Write the part of speech of the word in **bold**: *noun*, *verb*, or *adjective*.

1 **Nutrition** is the food we eat and its effect on our health and performance. _____

2 Most people need around 2,000 **calories**. _____

3 This is the energy a **typical** person uses in a day. _____

4 However, this **number** is different for athletes. _____

5 They **spend** a lot of time exercising, so they need to eat more. _____

6 Put the words in the correct order. Then check your sentences by reading the text again.

1 sugar / too much / not good / is / for anyone

_____

2 need / healthy foods / they

_____

3 had / he / egg sandwiches

_____

4 calories / do athletes / how many / need

_____

5 ate / Michael Phelps / 12,000 calories a day

_____

REAL-WORLD ENGLISH: Ordering food and drink;
complaining about service ▶4.4

1 @ Watch the video and choose *True* or *False*.

	True	False
1 The server's greeting is not polite.	☐	☐
2 Kevin uses a question to make his order.	☐	☐
3 Max asks a question about the food.	☐	☐
4 Andy complains about his food.	☐	☐
5 The server apologizes about the food.	☐	☐

2 Choose the correct word or phrase to complete the conversation politely.

A: Hi, what can I get for you?
B: ¹*I'll have / Give me* the soup of the day.
A: Good choice. The tomato soup is really good.
C: ²*Excuse me / Wait*, are there other vegetables in the tomato soup?
A: Let's see. No, I don't think so, but there is a little cream added.
B: Oh, then no cream for me ³*please / alright*.
A: Sure. One tomato soup with no cream, and have you decided?
C: ⁴*I'll have a salad. / Yeah, salad.*
D: ⁵*Hey / Excuse me*, can you come over here?
A: Sure. ⁶*Is everything OK? / What's up?*
D: ⁷*I'm sorry, but / This is wrong*, the soup doesn't taste like tomato. I think it's squash or something like that.
A: My apologies. I'll take care of that.

3 Complete the conversations between the server and customer with appropriate language.

1 Server: _____
  Customer: Can I have a diet soda, please?

2 Customer: _____
  Server: Yes, what can I get you?

3 Customer: _____
  Server: Yes, there are nuts in the pasta, but we can make it without nuts.

4 Customer: _____
  Server: Oh, I'm so sorry for the mixup. I'll return the fish and be back with your pizza right away!

5 Server: Hi. What can I get you today?
  Customer: _____

26 Unit 4 Extremes

UNIT REVIEW: Podcast

 Go online to listen to the podcast from the Unit Review.

1 Listen to the Unit Review Podcast. Choose *Yes* or *No*.

	Yes	No
1 Melanie is a kid.	☐	☐
2 Melanie skateboards on her neighborhood streets.	☐	☐
3 A few kids skateboard at the park.	☐	☐
4 Falling off your skateboard is OK.	☐	☐
5 Other kids want you to do well.	☐	☐

2 Listen again, and complete the sentences.

1 There are _____ kids trying out _____ of things.

2 Ride the ramps, jump _____ walls…

3 It sounds _____ scary.

4 It's why it's exciting. You try _____.

5 You always get back _____ the board.

LISTENING SKILL: Understanding incomplete speech ▶4.3

3 Listen to the extracts from the Unit Podcast. What do Melanie's answers to each question mean?

1 a Yeah, there are a lot of kids there. b Yeah, there are a lot of cool kids.

2 a I want to ride the ramps and jump over walls. b I ride the ramps and jump over walls.

3 a I fall a lot of times. b I don't fall a lot.

4 a No, I'm not worried. b No, I am worried.

5 a They know you can't do it. b They understand it's difficult.

DISCUSSION BOARD PREPARATION

4 Look at the Unit 4 Review Discussion Point. Read the questions in the prompt. Then read the reply. Label the part of the reply that answers question 1 from the prompt.

5 When does the writer think variety is good?

_____

6 When does the writer think variety is bad?

_____

7 Do you think that Melanie from the Unit Podcast agrees with the student response? Why or why not?

_____

Unit 4 Review Discussion Point

1   Read the quote. Do you agree that variety is important? Why or why not?
    "Variety is the very spice of life. That gives it all its flavour."
    —William Cowper (British poet), selected from *The Oxford Dictionary of Quotations*, 8th ed.,
    edited by Elizabeth Knowles
2   When is variety good? And when can variety be bad?

Latest: **Adam Cheng**
one hour ago
I agree with the quote. I think variety is good most of the time. It's fun to do different things each day. It's boring when every day is the same. Variety is like a spice because spice makes food taste better and variety makes each day a little better, a little different. For example, you can walk a different way to class. I don't think the changes have to be big changes. Any change is good.
    There are times when variety is bad. I read an article about food. When you eat lots of different foods at one meal, you eat more. It's better to cook a few things. Then you don't eat too much food. However, if you prepare lots of things, then you want to try them all. There's lots of variety, so you eat too much.

8   Overall, did the writer answer all the questions? If yes, explain. If no, what can the writer change?

_____

_____

9   Review the rubric. Use the rubric to give a score for the reply.
Give points: 0 (not successful)–10 (successful).

Writing a Discussion Board Post	Points
The post answers the questions clearly and completely.	
The post tells when variety is good and when it is bad.	
The writer uses the correct parts of speech.	
The writer uses quantifiers correctly with countable and uncountable nouns.	
The post uses *there is / there are* correctly.	
The post is long enough (100–150 words).	
Total	

WRITE YOUR POST

10 Read the quote. Do you agree that variety is important? Why or why not? Write a draft of your post for the Unit 4 Review Discussion Point.

"Variety is the very spice of life. That gives it all its flavour."
—William Cowper (British poet), selected from *The Oxford Dictionary of Quotations*,
8th ed., edited by Elizabeth Knowles

11 Use the rubric from Exercise 9 to score your post. Then improve your post.

Go online to add your comments to the discussion board.

5 Creativity

Present continuous ▶5.1

1 Complete the sentences with the present continuous of the **bold** verb.

1 He **designs** jewelry.   He'<u>'s designing jewelry</u>.

2 She **makes** cards.   She'<u>_____</u>.

3 They **work** together.   They'<u>_____</u>.

4 We **study** English.   We'<u>_____</u>.

5 You **go** to design school.   You'<u>_____</u>.

6 Sara **takes** classes.   Sara'<u>_____</u>.

2 Use the verbs from the box to write positive (+) and negative (–) sentences in the present continuous.

make	talk	have	go	~~shop~~	start

1 I / for a new coat at my favorite store. +

<u>I am shopping for a new coat at my favorite store.</u>

2 He / jewelry for his friends and family. +

_____

3 She / a new business. –

_____

4 We / a great time at the art museum. +

_____

5 You / to class today. –

_____

6 They / about the exhibit. –

_____

Verbs + *to* infinitive ▶5.2

3 Find the extra word in each sentence.

1 We to plan to start our own business.

2 I would to like to improve my language skills.

3 She wants to design to women's clothing.

4 We to decided to study engineering.

5 They need to to create a project for class.

6 We to like to go to the art museum.

4 Match the beginning of the sentence in A with the ending in B.

A

1 On the weekend, I like   ____

2 I can't meet today. I need   ____

3 Because I love clothing, I want to   ____

4 He needs money, so he decided   ____

5 I am so tired! I would like to   ____

6 She loves French food. She wants to   ____

B

a become a fashion designer.

b to get in the car and drive somewhere new.

c sleep for 20 hours!

d to get a job at the museum café.

e to prepare for a presentation tomorrow.

f take cooking classes.

Simple present and present continuous ▶5.3

5 Choose *P* (present) or *PC* (present continuous).

		P	PC
1	We love Picasso!	☐	☐
2	We want to buy a painting.	☐	☐
3	Are you selling anything?	☐	☐
4	What are you doing tonight?	☐	☐
5	We're talking about the price.	☐	☐
6	Are you OK with the price?	☐	☐

6 Use the correct verb to complete each sentence.

1 I _____ about buying the painting.

am thinking / think

2 Are you _____ to the art show tonight?

go / going

3 Is he _____ any paintings?

sell / selling

4 The artist _____ right there. Should we talk to him?

stands / is standing

5 I really _____ the colors in this painting.

like / am liking

6 She _____ like the woman in the painting!

looks / is looking

Hobbies ▶5.1

1 Write the correct phrase under each picture.

bake and decorate cakes	build crafts	go online
design my own clothes	make a machine	

1 _____ 2 _____ 3 _____

4 _____ 5 _____

2 Rewrite part of the sentence. Use the phrases in the box with the same meaning.

build furniture	bake cakes and cookies
grow plants and vegetables in	~~make jewelry~~
buy things online	

1 I design necklaces and earrings. ___make jewelry___

2 I make desserts and other sweet treats.

_____

3 I create chairs and tables. _____

4 I water and take care of my garden.

_____

5 I order things off the Internet. _____

Skills ▶5.2

3 Match a word in A to a word in B and complete the sentences.

A

develop	design	organize	decorate	write

B

cakes	events	stories	clothes	programs

1 I own a bakery. I _____ and sell them.

2 I plan and _____ for my company. Tomorrow we have a picnic and baseball game.

3 I am a software engineer. I _____ and apps for computers and phones.

4 I work in fashion. I _____ for men.

5 I'm a writer. I _____ for children.

4 What is the person good at? Write the phrase.

decorating homes	designing jewelry
improving skills	developing programs
~~organizing events~~	

1 "I like to plan weddings." ___organizing events___

2 "I'm working hard and getting better at writing."

_____

3 "Ali is creating some really cool apps." _____

4 "Li is painting the living room and hanging pictures on the wall." _____

5 "Jen is drawing pictures of necklaces. She is going to make them." _____

VOCABULARY DEVELOPMENT: Time expressions ▶5.3

5 Complete the sentences with a time expression.

1 U_____ I stay up late working.

2 T_____ I'm working with Fernando.

3 R_____ now I'm busy.

4 S_____ I drink coffee at night.

5 A_____ the moment, I'm not doing anything.

6 Are the time expressions used correctly? Write Y (yes) or N (no).

_____ 1 Today, he's at his job.

_____ 2 I always am working on Saturday.

_____ 3 I usually am writing a book.

_____ 4 At the moment, I'm reading.

_____ 5 He never is cooking.

READING SKILL: Recognizing and understanding cause and effect linking words: *Because, as, so* ▶5.1

1 Choose the best word to show cause and effect.

1 *Because / So* writing well is important for many jobs, it's taught at school.
2 *Because / Because of* machines can do many jobs, workers need to improve their thinking skills.
3 *So / As* many jobs are changing, our classrooms should change, too.
4 Teaching creativity is not easy, *so / because* we need to help teachers.
5 Students need more time to work together, *so / because* classes need to be longer.

2 Is the part in **bold** the cause or the effect? Choose *Cause* or *Effect*.

	Cause	Effect
1 **Because of robots**, workers now need to be creative.	☐	☐
2 They need to work together, so **they can do jobs that machines can't**.	☐	☐
3 **As workers need these skills**, our classrooms need to teach them.	☐	☐
4 **In teams, students ask questions and solve problems** so they improve their thinking and communication skills.	☐	☐
5 We need to let students fail and try again, so **they learn to think on their own**.	☐	☐

READING: Practice

3 Read the text. Find a skill in each paragraph.

Teach the Skills We Need

These days, we hear a lot about robots and machines. We understand they can do many jobs. Because of robots, workers now need to be creative. They need to think in different ways, so they can do jobs that machines can't. As workers need these skills, our classrooms need to teach them. However, right now we are teaching facts, not thinking.

Teachers need to have students work in teams. In teams, students ask questions and solve problems, so they improve their thinking and communication skills. However, creativity is not easy to teach or test, so we need to help teachers. We need to design our classrooms, so students can make choices. We need to let students fail and try again, so they learn to think on their own.

—adapted from *A Dictionary of Education*, 2nd ed., edited by Susan Wallace

4 Choose the best answer.

1 What does the author of the article want?

   a   to change teaching

   b   to use robots

2 Who is the audience of the article?

   a   workers

   b   everyone

3 What does the author think?

   a   We are preparing students correctly.

   b   We are preparing students incorrectly.

4 What does the author think about robots?

   a   They are not good.

   b   They can do many jobs.

5 What does the author think is important?

   a   teaching thinking skills

   b   teaching important facts

5 Write the correct word from the text.

1 Because of r_____, we need to teach differently.

2 W_____ need to do jobs that robots can't do.

3 We need to let s_____ fail.

4 We need to help t_____ so they can change the classroom.

5 We teach f_____, but we need to teach thinking skills.

6 Write *T* (True) or *F* (False).

_____ 1 Work now is different from the past.

_____ 2 It's easy to teach creativity.

_____ 3 It's important to think the same as others.

_____ 4 Schools right now are teaching in creative ways.

_____ 5 Robots do not have a big effect on our world.

REAL-WORLD ENGLISH: Asking for and giving opinions and advice ▶5.4

1 🔄 Watch the video, and match the questions with the correct opinions.

Do you like them?	What do you think about the class trip to the art museum tomorrow?
What do you think about it?	What's your opinion of the Impressionists?
What's your opinion?	

1 _____

I'm excited to see the Mary Cassatt exhibit. I think she's really interesting.

2 _____

I hate it! It's *so* boring! I don't understand why it's so popular.

3 _____

Oh, I'm really looking forward to it.

4 _____

I think they're wonderful!

5 _____

Yeah, they're great!

2 🔄 Listen for the phrases in the video. Does the speaker's tone match the opinion? Choose *Yes* or *No*.

		Yes	No
1	I'm excited to see the Mary Cassatt exhibit.	☐	☐
2	I hate it! It's so boring!	☐	☐
3	Oh, I'm really looking forward to it.	☐	☐
4	I'm excited, too!	☐	☐
5	To be honest, they're not my favorite.	☐	☐

3 Put the words in correct order to ask questions or make sentences for opinions.

1 think / what / you / own business / about / do / managing your

   What do you think about managing your own business _____?

2 your / are / classes at night / in / a good idea / opinion

   _____?

3 excited / to do / I'm / group projects

   _____.

4 to art museums / like to / I / go / to be honest / don't

   _____.

5 your / Impressionist art / what's / opinion / on

   _____?

LISTENING SKILL: Recognizing weak sounds ▶5.3

1 🔊 Listen. Compete the sentences with the unstressed words.

1 Miriam, what are you working _____ now?

2 And I'm interested _____ the world, _____ there is always something _____ write about.

3 Then I see how all _____ poems fit together.

4 _____ what _____ this book about?

5 _____ book _____ called *Build Your Own*.

UNIT REVIEW: Podcast

📲 **Go online to listen to the podcast from the Unit Review.**

2 🔊 Listen to the Unit Review Podcast. Choose the correct answer.

1 What number book is Miriam working on?
   a 8   b 7

2 Where do Miriam's ideas come from?
   a an interest in the world   b reading other books

3 In the middle of writing one poem, what happens?
   a she gets another idea   b she can't think of more ideas

4 What is her new book about?
   a teaching   b our culture

3 🔊 Listen again. Write *T* (True) or *F* (False).

____ 1 At the moment, Miriam is working on a poetry class.

____ 2 Miriam thinks it is not easy to think of ideas.

____ 3 Miriam's poems tell us to take classes and read books to be better.

____ 4 Miriam is a poet and professor.

____ 5 Miriam's book is about not doing things.

DISCUSSION BOARD PREPARATION

4 Look at the Unit 5 Review Discussion Point. Read the questions in the prompt. Then read the reply. Label the part of the reply that explains what the quote means.

5 Does the student agree with the quote? What example does the student use to support her opinion?

_____

_____

6 Why does the writer talk about worrying?

_____

7 Read the last two sentences. Are they good closing sentences? Why or why not?

_____

Unit 5 Review Discussion Point

1   Read the quote. What do you think it means? Do you think it's true?
    "You can't use up creativity. The more you use, the more you have."
    —Maya Angelou, 1928–2014, American writer, selected from *Oxford Essential Quotations*, 4ᵗʰ ed.
2   Give an example from your life to explain your answer.

Latest: **Adela Sibiu**
one hour ago
I think the quote means if you develop ideas, then you have more and more ideas. It's a cause and effect relationship. The cause is thinking, and the effect is more ideas. I think it's true. For example, right now Im writing my ideas. It's not easy. I would like to write something interesting, but I don't know what to say. I'm thinking and writing and as I do, it's getting easier. I think the quote is true, but you can't worry too much. If you worry about your ideas, then it's hard to develop more. However, if you are thinking and writing it all down and not worrying, then it's easy to be creative. Later you can see if your ideas are good or not!

8   Overall, did the writer answer all the questions? If yes, explain. If no, what can the writer change?

_____

_____

9   Review the rubric. Use the rubric to give a score for the reply.
Give points: 0 (not successful)–10 (successful).

Writing a Discussion Board Post	Points
The post answers the questions clearly and completely.	
The post tells what the quote means.	
The writer tells if he or she agrees with the quote.	
The writer gives an example to explain her answer.	
The writer uses the present continuous and verbs + *to* infinitive correctly.	
The post is long enough (100–150 words).	
Total	

WRITE YOUR POST

10   Read the quote. What do you think it means? Do you think it's true? Write your post for the discussion board.

   "You can't use up creativity. The more you use, the more you have."
—Maya Angelou, 1928–2014, American writer, selected from
Oxford Essential Quotations, 4ᵗʰ ed.

11   Use the rubric from Exercise 9 to score your post. Then improve your post.

   Go online to add your comments to the discussion board.

6 Places

Have to and *don't have to* ▶6.1

1 Write questions to match the answers.

1 A: <u>Does she have to go to the mall tonight?</u>

B: Yes, she has to go to the mall tonight.

2 A: _____?

B: No, he doesn't have to get his hair cut.

3 A: _____?

B: Yes, she has to leave at 8.

4 A: _____?

B: Yes, I have to wake up early at 5:30.

5 A: _____?

B: No, we don't have to go to the museum.

2 Correct the incorrect sentences.

1 We doesn't have to go the grocery store.

_____

2 Does you have to stop at the ATM?

_____

3 I don't have to study at the library tonight.

_____

4 Do she have to work at the bakery today?

_____

5 He don't have to go to the gym right now.

_____

Can for possibility ▶6.2

3 Complete the conversations with *can* or *can't*.

1 A: _____ you relax at night?

B: No, I _____. I often have to work at night.

2 A: _____ you go with me on the tour?

B: No, I _____. I'm sorry. I'm busy.

3 A: Where _____ I get a cup of coffee?

B: You _____ get one across the street.

4 A: Who _____ drive to the movie tonight?

B: I _____, but Sara probably _____.

4 Use the verbs in the box to write positive (+) and negative (–) sentences with *can*.

buy	call	eat	relax	afford	drive

1 You / a ticket to London for $120! +

<u>You can buy a ticket to London for $120.</u>

2 I / a $3,000 12-day European tour! –

_____

3 We / on a beach in the sun in Portugal. +

_____

4 She / a car in this country. –

_____

5 He / his parents from the hotel. +

_____

6 You / a cheap meal in this city. –

_____

Should / Shouldn't: Advice ▶6.3

5 Choose the best answer.

1 We *should / shouldn't* go on a trip in December. It's too cold to travel to Europe then.

2 We *should / shouldn't* go in the summer. The tickets are cheaper in the winter. It's a better time to travel.

3 You *should / shouldn't* stay here with your family. Then you can be with them for your birthday.

4 I *should / shouldn't* see a new place. I am always here on my breaks. I want to do something new.

5 You *should / shouldn't* just think of yourself. Think of your family. They want you to be with them.

6 I *should / shouldn't* go abroad. Then my family can come visit me! They love to travel too!

6 Complete the sentences using the cues in parentheses and *should* or *shouldn't*.

1 You look tired. You _____. (relax)

2 It's getting late. We _____ home. (go)

3 The price is high. You _____ the ticket. (not / buy)

4 The city is too busy in summer. He _____ then. (not / visit)

5 She enjoys learning. She _____ language classes. (take)

Places ▶6.1

1 Match the statements with the advice.

1 I need a haircut. ____

2 I need a new job. I should work ____
   at a clothing store. I like fashion.

3 I love to shop! I like lots of different stores. ____

4 I need milk, butter, and eggs. ____

a We should go to the mall and look around at the different stores there!

b You should go to my hairdresser. He's great.

c You should go to the store now. It closes at 9.

d You should go to the department store. They are hiring salespeople.

2 Choose the correct place.

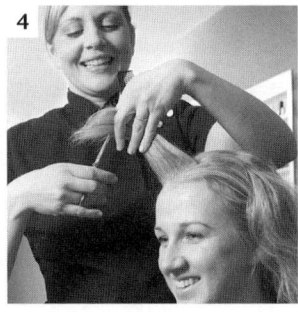

1 I shop for food at the *farmer's market / bakery*.

2 I walk around the *shopping mall / grocery store*.

3 I buy clothes at the *gym / department store*.

4 I like my *hairdresser / bakery*. She does a good job.

3 Use the phrases in the box to replace the **bold** words.

adventure	can't afford	~~go abroad~~	relax	view

1 I want to **travel** and see the world.

   go abroad

2 I like **excitement** and doing new things.

   _____

3 I **don't have the money for** the trip.

   _____

4 I want to lie on a beach and **rest** all day.

   _____

5 Look out the window! What beautiful **sight**!

   _____

Vacation ▶6.2

4 Choose the correct words to complete the paragraph.

I love to travel and really want to go ¹*abroad / afford*. I want to go to Japan, but I'd go anywhere for an exciting ²*tour / adventure*. That's the most important part. I don't need to ³*relax / afford*. On vacation, I don't want to sit on a beach with a beautiful ⁴*view / tour*. I want to see the city. I'd love to go on a food ⁵*tour / view* and try different foods. I'm saving my money, so I can ⁶*relax / afford* the trip!

VOCABULARY DEVELOPMENT:
Adverbs of manner ▶6.3

5 Complete the sentences with a word from the box.

carefully	slowly	loudly	quietly

1 Small children walk _____. They don't have long legs, so it's hard for them to go fast.

2 Please talk _____ in the library. People are working.

3 The man in the front of the bus is talking _____. Everyone can hear him.

4 Walk _____. It is wet. I don't want you to fall.

6 Complete the sentences with the opposite of the **bold** word.

1 You're talking too **loudly**. You're talking too _____.

2 You run so **quickly**. You run so _____.

3 He went home **sadly**. He went home _____.

4 You drive **slowly**. You drive _____.

5 He set his glass down **without care**, and it broke. He _____ set his glass down.

READING SKILL: Scanning for specific information ▶6.2

1 Scan the text. Match the questions to the answers from the text.

____ 1 For how many years have people used cruise ships?

____ 2 What year was the first cruise?

____ 3 How many people were on the first cruise?

____ 4 Where did the British company's ship go?

____ 5 What was the most popular place to go on a cruise in 2004?

a 80

b over 150

c Norway

d the Caribbean

e 1833

2 Scan the text. Correct the incorrect part of the sentence.

1 The first cruise went from Sicily to Istanbul. _from Naples to Istanbul_

2 By the 1970s, a British company was making regular trips to Norway. _____

3 In 2004, the most popular cruises were to Naples. _____

4 By 2015, the smallest ship had 6,296 people on it. _____

5 The least popular cruises were to the Caribbean. _____

READING: Practice

3 Read the text. What detail is the most surprising?

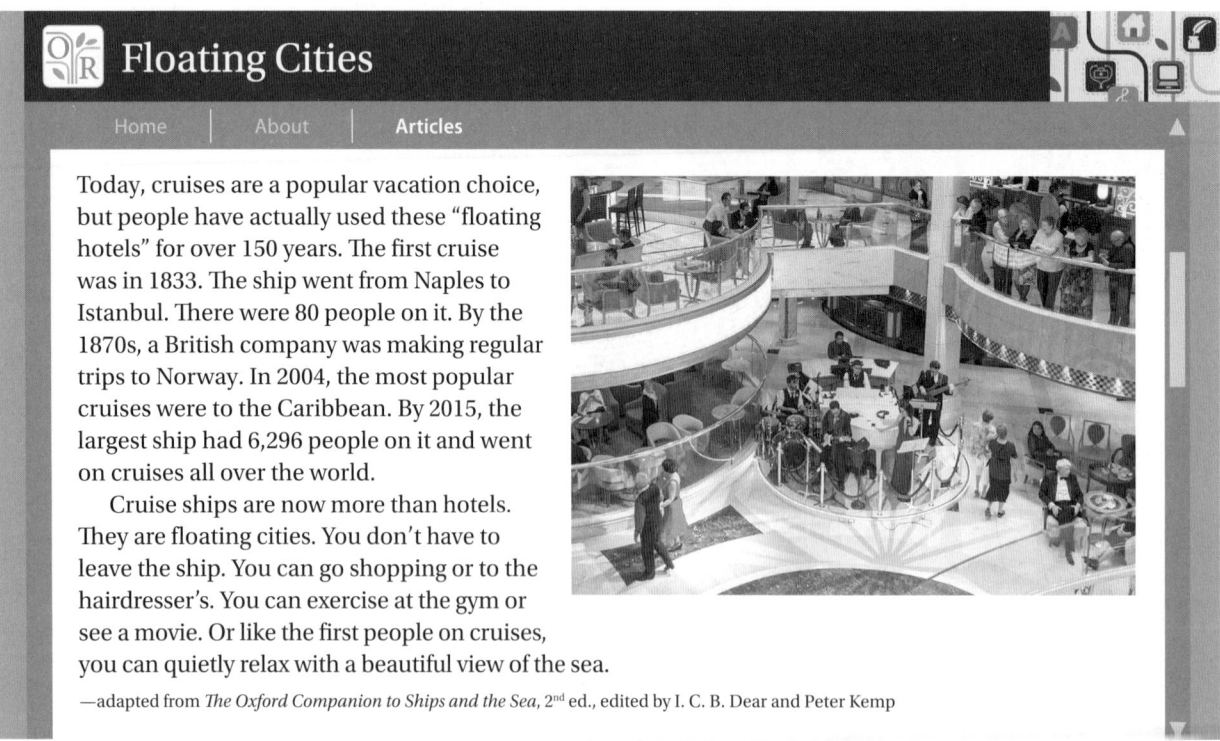

Floating Cities

Home | About | **Articles**

Today, cruises are a popular vacation choice, but people have actually used these "floating hotels" for over 150 years. The first cruise was in 1833. The ship went from Naples to Istanbul. There were 80 people on it. By the 1870s, a British company was making regular trips to Norway. In 2004, the most popular cruises were to the Caribbean. By 2015, the largest ship had 6,296 people on it and went on cruises all over the world.

Cruise ships are now more than hotels. They are floating cities. You don't have to leave the ship. You can go shopping or to the hairdresser's. You can exercise at the gym or see a movie. Or like the first people on cruises, you can quietly relax with a beautiful view of the sea.

—adapted from *The Oxford Companion to Ships and the Sea*, 2nd ed., edited by I. C. B. Dear and Peter Kemp

Unit 6 Places

4 Number the events in the order from the text. The first and last are numbered for you.

_____ One cruise ship has 6,296 people on it.

_____ The most popular cruise is to the Caribbean.

_1_ The first cruise happens.

_5_ You can go to the hairdresser's on a cruise ship.

_____ A British company begins making cruise trips.

5 What things can you do on a cruise ship? Choose *Yes* or *No*.

		Yes	No
1	Go shopping	☐	☐
2	Go on a guided tour	☐	☐
3	Relax and enjoy the view	☐	☐
4	Go to the hairdresser's	☐	☐
5	See a movie	☐	☐
6	Go to a farmer's market	☐	☐
7	Go to the gym	☐	☐

6 Write *T* (True) or *F* (False).

_____ 1 The purpose of the text is to get people to go on a cruise.

_____ 2 The writer talks about her trip on a cruise ship.

_____ 3 The writer was on the first cruise.

_____ 4 The text gives the history of cruise ships.

_____ 5 The writer thinks there are not many things to do on a cruise.

REAL-WORLD ENGLISH: Giving, accepting, and rejecting advice ▶6.4

1 🔘 Watch the video and choose the correct words.

1 Max: You *should / could* come with me!

2 Max: No … I mean you *should / could* come to London.

3 Max: Well, the flights to the UK are pretty cheap right now. You *should / could* think about it.

4 Max: My uncle has an international law firm in London. You *should / could* probably get an internship there.

5 Andy: Really? Wow. That sounds good. Oh…but where *would / should* I stay?

2 Read the advice. Is the response Polite or Rude?

You should study French so you can go to France.   **Polite**   **Rude**

1 Maybe, I'll try that.   ☐   ☐

2 No way.   ☐   ☐

3 What? Never.   ☐   ☐

4 That could be fun.   ☐   ☐

5 Well, I don't think I can take another language class.   ☐   ☐

3 Match the advice in A with the response to accept (+) or reject (–).

_____ 1 You should go to the doctor. –   a OK! Let's look for a birthday gift for Mom.

_____ 2 You should go to Japan on your break. –   b Well, I think I'll be OK in a day or two.

_____ 3 Well, we could go shopping at the mall. +   c That's a good idea, but can we go another time?

_____ 4 Let's walk over to the farmer's market. –   d That's a great idea! I can't wait to try it.

_____ 5 You should study for the test tomorrow. –   e That's a good idea, but I can't afford the ticket.

_____ 6 Let's see. What about Thai food? We could   f That's OK. I am ready for it.
            go to the new Thai restaurant. +

4 Rewrite the sentences with the words in parentheses and *should* to give advice.

1 Talk more loudly. (our teacher)

   _____

2 Walk more slowly. (tour guide)

   _____

3 Drive carefully. (bus driver)

   _____

4 Walk faster. (you)

   _____

5 Save more money. (he)

   _____

6 Visit the art museum. (we)

   _____

UNIT REVIEW: Podcast

Go online to listen to the podcast from the Unit Review.

1 Listen to the Unit Review Podcast. Correct the incorrect statements.

1 Mr. Menendez is a teacher.

_____

2 The school gives tours.

_____

3 You can't relax at the beach.

_____

4 Most people don't like the tours.

_____

2 Listen again. Complete the sentences with the words you hear.

1 You d_____ spend all your time in classes.

2 It's y_____ vacation.

3 Then they can more e_____ explore the city.

4 And you can q_____ learn the language when you spend time with the people.

LISTENING SKILL: Listening for details ▶6.1

3 Read the questions. Listen again to the podcast. Then match the questions to the answers.

_____ 1 Who are the classes for?   a in the afternoon

_____ 2 When are the classes?   b Spanish

_____ 3 Where are the classes?   c in the morning

_____ 4 What kind of classes are at the school? d Puerto Rico

_____ 5 When are the tours?   e tourists

DISCUSSION BOARD PREPARATION

4 Look at the Unit 6 Review Discussion Point. Read the questions in the prompt. Then read the reply. Label the parts of the reply that answer questions 1 and 2.

5 Has the writer visited a country without knowing the language? What does the writer say about this?

_____

_____

6 What examples does the writer use to tell why she disagrees?

_____

7 What advice does the writer give?

_____

Unit 6   Places   41

Unit 6 Review Discussion Point

1   Read the quote. Do you agree or disagree with it? Have you visited a country without knowing the language?
"No man should travel until he has learned the language of the country he visits."
—Ralph Waldo Emerson (American writer), selected from *Oxford Dictionary of American Quotations*, 2nd ed., edited by Hugh Rawson and Margaret Miner

2   Explain your opinion.

Latest: Jingxian Chang
one hour ago
I agree with it. I think people should always learn the language before they visit a new country. I visited the United States last year. I took English classes, but it was still difficult for me! You need to talk to people in the country you go to. You have to ask for directions. You have to order food from a menu. I did not know these things, and it was not good. You also can't safely visit a new place without knowing the language. If you have a problem, you have to ask for help. I knew some English, but I could not easily talk with others. You should join an online group and practice before you go abroad! Then you can learn quickly, and you can feel better about your speaking.

8   Overall, did the writer answer all the questions? If yes, explain. If no, what can the writer change?

_____

_____

9   Review the rubric. Use the rubric to give a score for the reply.
Give points: 0 (not successful)–10 (successful).

Writing a Discussion Board Post	Points
The post answers the questions completely and clearly.	
The writer tells if he or she agrees and explains her opinion.	
The writer uses adverbs of manner correctly.	
The writer uses *have to* and *don't have to* correctly.	
The writer uses *should* and *shouldn't* to give advice.	
The post is long enough (100–150 words).	
Total	

WRITE YOUR POST

10   Read the quote. Do you agree or disagree with it? Have you visited a country without knowing the language? Write a draft of your post for the Unit 6 Review Discussion Point.

"No man should travel until he has learned the language of the country he visits."
—Ralph Waldo Emerson, (American writer), selected from *Oxford Dictionary of American Quotations*, 2nd ed., edited by Hugh Rawson and Margaret Miner

11   Use the rubric from Exercise 9 to score your post. Then improve your post.

 Go online to add your comments to the discussion board.

7 People

Simple past: *Be* ▶7.1

1 Complete the sentences with *was* or *were*.

1 Valentina Tereshkova _____ the first woman to go to space.

2 In 1962, she and three other women _____ in a program in Russia to prepare for space travel.

3 At the time, there _____ not a lot of programs for women.

4 In 1896, Dimitirios Loundras _____ the youngest person in the Olympics. He _____ ten years old!

5 There _____ many other young people in the Olympics in the past. At the Olympics, you can be any age!

2 Write positive (+) and negative (–) sentences with *was* or *were*.

1 I / a teacher in Jordan +

_____

2 We / happy about the test on Monday –

_____

3 They / in Prague a couple years ago +

_____

4 He / a famous actor –

_____

5 She / a wonderful writer –

_____

Simple past: Regular and irregular verbs ▶7.2

3 Write the simple past form of the verbs.

1 go _____

2 visit _____

3 know _____

4 watch _____

5 learn _____

6 become _____

7 has _____

8 love _____

9 get _____

10 live _____

4 Correct the mistakes in the simple past verbs.

1 Shakespeare writed more than 150 poems and 35 plays. _____

2 King Henry VIII married Anne Boleyn, and they haved a daughter, Elizabeth, in 1558. _____

3 She was a famous queen. She die in 1603. She was 45 years old. _____

4 The writer Jhumpa Lahiri win a famous award in 2000 for her writing. _____

5 When she was young, her teacher can't say her name—Nilanjana Sudeshna—so she called her by her nickname, Jhumpa. _____

Simple past questions ▶7.3

5 Match the questions with the correct responses.

Why did you move?	Did you get a job?
What did you study?	Did you like Madrid?
Did you like college?	Where did you move to?

1 _____

Because I wanted to go to college abroad.

2 _____

Yes, I did, but I wanted to go somewhere new.

3 _____

Buenos Aires, Argentina.

4 _____

Business management.

5 _____

No, I didn't enjoy my classes.

6 _____

Yes, I worked at the writing center at school.

VOCABULARY

6 Write the words in the correct order to make questions using the simple past.

1 you / play / What / did / you were / a child / when

_____

2 like / Did / to draw / were / when you / you / small

_____

3 enjoy / What / you / about school / did

_____

4 move / when you / Did / you / were younger

_____

VOCABULARY DEVELOPMENT:
Time expressions ▶7.1

1 Find the time expressions. Write them in the blanks.

1 I worked on my project last night.

_____

2 I was born on August 8, 1988. _____

3 In the 1900s, my grandparents and their families moved to India. _____

4 Last year, my brother completed college.

_____

5 Two years ago, my cousin married a famous actor.

_____

6 In 2016, I traveled to Barcelona for the wedding.

_____

2 Match a word or words in A to a word or words in B to complete the sentences below.

A

last	two	on	in	in the

B

weeks ago	night	Tuesday	2017	late 1800s

1 I couldn't sleep _____. I'm really tired today.

2 I finished my classes _____. After that, I went to Australia for ten days.

3 I started college _____. In that same year, my brother moved to Korea.

4 My mother's grandparents moved to India

_____ — a long time ago.

5 I went out to dinner and saw my parents

_____. The day before was my father's birthday.

3 Correct the incorrect sentences.

1 Brian Lara was a great cricket player in the late 1990s and early 2000s.

_____

2 Brian Lara played an amazing cricket match on 1999.

_____

3 He played his last match in April 21, 2007.

_____

4 When he was in Trinidad, I saw him play.

_____

5 I visited Trinidad ten years go.

_____

Verbs ▶7.2

4 Complete the sentences.

1 He did a good job. He won an award. He _____.

2 He didn't do well. He _____ the test.

3 Her family always _____ her.

4 The scientists _____ ice on the planet.

5 They _____ on this day two years ago!

6 Isabel _____ a doctor last year.

5 Match the beginning of the sentence in A with the ending in B.

A

1 He succeeded at work _____

2 His parents encouraged him _____

3 Nazar failed his law exam _____

4 Josef discovered another way
  to solve the math problem _____

5 He became a doctor _____

B

a because he thought about it for a long time.

b because he was a good manager.

c to be a good student.

d because he arrived late.

e to help sick children.

READING SKILL: Finding main ideas ▶7.2

1 Read the title and the first and last sentences. Complete the sentences with the correct words.

1 The text is about r_____ stories.

2 The writer really likes r_____.

3 In the story, women s_____.

2 Read the article. Choose the main idea.

a The best book is *Hidden Figures: The American Dream and the Untold Story of the Black Women Mathematicians Who Helped Win the Space Race.*

b The 1940s through the 1960s was not an easy time for women in the United States.

c True stories about people's lives are better than stories writers create.

d Good writers read real stories.

e People should read stories by Joan Didion.

READING: Practice

3 Read the blog. Do you agree with the writer? Why or why not?

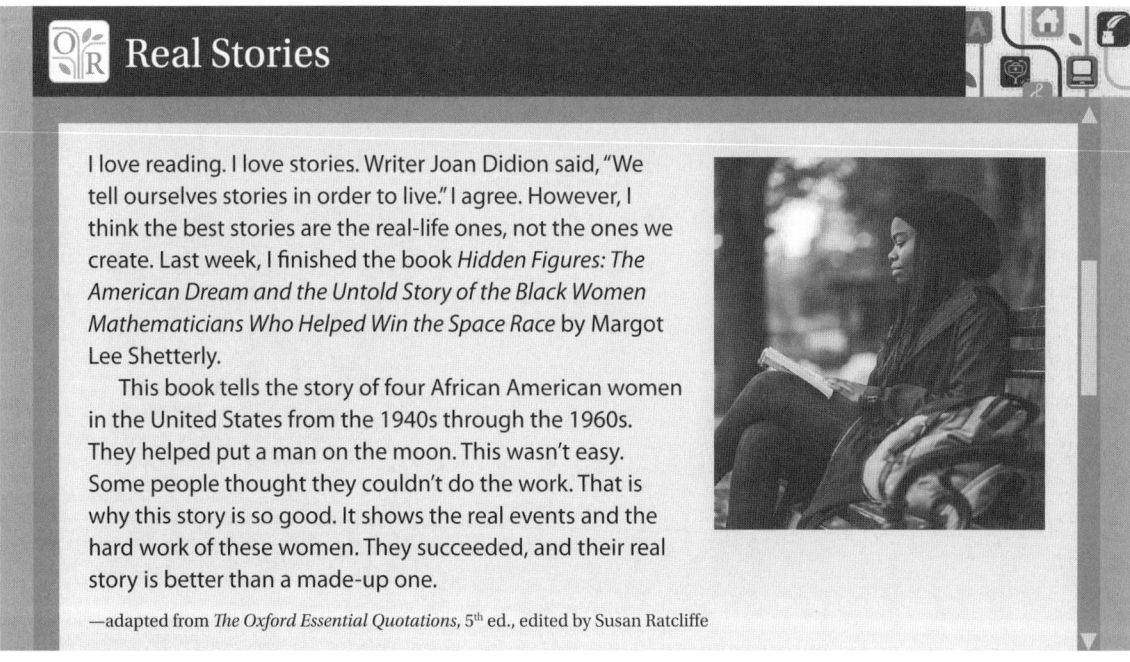

Real Stories

I love reading. I love stories. Writer Joan Didion said, "We tell ourselves stories in order to live." I agree. However, I think the best stories are the real-life ones, not the ones we create. Last week, I finished the book *Hidden Figures: The American Dream and the Untold Story of the Black Women Mathematicians Who Helped Win the Space Race* by Margot Lee Shetterly.

This book tells the story of four African American women in the United States from the 1940s through the 1960s. They helped put a man on the moon. This wasn't easy. Some people thought they couldn't do the work. That is why this story is so good. It shows the real events and the hard work of these women. They succeeded, and their real story is better than a made-up one.

—adapted from *The Oxford Essential Quotations*, 5ᵗʰ ed., edited by Susan Ratcliffe

4 Correct the incorrect sentences.

1 The writer of the blog wrote *Hidden Figures: The American Dream and the Untold Story of the Black Women Mathematicians Who Helped Win the Space Race.*

_____

2 The book tells the story of four African American women in the United States from the 1940s through the 1960s.

_____

3 Some people thought the women could not do the work.

_____

4 The women helped put a woman on the moon.

_____

5 The women in the story were teachers.

_____

6 The women's work was easy for them.

_____

5 Write short answers to the questions.

1 What author does the blog writer quote?

_____

2 Who wrote the book?

_____

3 What makes the book so good?

_____

4 Where do the events happen?

_____

5 Who are the people in the book?

_____

6 When did the events happen?

_____

6 What does the writer think? Choose *Agree* or *Disagree*.

	Agree	Disagree
1 Other people should read the book.	☐	☐
2 People should read more made-up stories.	☐	☐
3 Writing real stories is important.	☐	☐
4 The book could have been better.	☐	☐
5 The women in the book failed.	☐	☐
6 Good stories are about success through hard work.	☐	☐

REAL-WORLD ENGLISH: Thanking and responding ▶7.4

1 @ Watch the video. Write the response to each statement. Then write *formal* or *for any situation* to describe it.

	Response	Formal or For Any Situation?
1 Oh … could you get me some tea?		
2 Thanks for meeting with me.		
3 Thanks a lot, Professor Lopez.		
4 OK, thanks for your time, Professor. I really appreciate it.		

2 Complete the dialogue between a professor and a student with words from the box.

appreciate	course	really	thanks	a lot

Student: Excuse me, do you have a minute, Professor Andrews?

Professor: Yes, of ¹_____.

Student: Great, ²_____. I am thinking about taking your writing class in the spring. I really like your short stories.

Professor: Thanks ³_____. I ⁴_____ that. We don't look at my stories in class, but we do read a lot of great writers from the 1900s to modern day. You should sign up. The class fills up fast.

Student: OK, great. Well, thanks for talking to me. I ⁵_____ appreciate it. I'm very excited about class!

3 Match the situations with the responses in the box.

No problem.	I really appreciate your time. I hope to hear from you.
Thanks.	Thank you SO MUCH. You are the BEST.
Thanks for explaining everything.	

1 Your friend picked you up from the airport. He had to wait two hours because your flight was late.

_____

2 The server at the café just gave you the coffee you ordered.

_____

3 You finished your interview and are shaking hands with the manager who interviewed you.

_____

4 You are leaving your professor's office. She answered questions about your homework.

_____

5 Your friend just thanked you for giving him change for a dollar.

_____

LISTENING SKILL: Understanding contrast linkers ▶7.3

1 🔊 Listen to the sentences. Write the contrast linker you hear.

1 _____

2 _____

3 _____

4 _____

5 _____

UNIT REVIEW: Podcast

🔇 **Go online to listen to the podcast from the Unit Review.**

2 🔊 Listen to the Unit Review Podcast. Choose the correct answer.

1 What is special about Hilde?
  a she is a young writer   b she is a young kid

2 What did her mother encourage her to do?
  a write stories   b ask questions

3 How did Hilde learn about writing news stories?
  a she learned at school   b she learned on trips with her dad

4 What did Hilde discover about her mom?
  a her plan for a new car   b her plan for a gift for her dad

5 Is everyone happy about Hilde's writing?
  a yes   b no

3 🔊 Listen again. Correct the sentences.

1 Hilde is ~~eleven~~ years old.   _____ten_____

2 Hilde's mom was a news writer.   _____

3 Hilde writes stories about news in her house.   _____

4 Hilde thinks she should be playing with toys.   _____

5 Hilde thinks people let kids do anything they want.   _____

DISCUSSION BOARD PREPARATION

4 Look at the Unit 7 Review Discussion Point. Read the questions in the prompt. Then read the reply. Label the sentence that best states the main idea.

5 What example does the writer use?

_____

6 What kind of person does the writer think changes the world?

_____

7 Do you think Hilde from the Unit Podcast agrees with the student? Why or why not?

_____

Unit 7 Review Discussion Point

1　Read the quote. What kind of person can change the world?
"The people who are crazy enough to think they can change the world are the ones who do."
—Apple computer Inc. TV ad, 1997, selected from *Oxford Dictionary of American Quotations*,
2nd ed., edited by Hugh Rawson and Margaret Miner

Latest: Theresa Munez
one hour ago
All kinds of people can change the world. I agree with Hilde that adults tell kids they can do anything but don't let them. However, kids can change the world. For example, my neighbor wanted people to drive more slowly down her street. A few years ago, her brother was almost hit by a car. After that, she asked people in our neighborhood to not drive fast. She put up signs, and it worked. She was only thirteen. So I don't think you have to be crazy to change the world. You just have to care, and most often the people that change the world had something happen to them. They don't get angry. Instead, they discover ways to make the world better, and sometimes they are kids, and sometimes they are adults.

8 Overall, did the writer answer all the questions? If yes, explain. If no, what can the writer change?

_____

_____

9 Review the rubric. Use the rubric to give a score for the reply.
Give points: 0 (not successful)–10 (successful).

Writing a Discussion Board Post	Points
The writer states the main idea of his or her reply.	
The writer answers the question clearly and completely.	
The writer developed his or her ideas with details.	
The writer uses simple past *be* correctly.	
The writer uses simple past regular and irregular verbs correctly.	
The post is long enough (100–150 words).	
Total	

WRITE YOUR POST

10 Read the quote. What kind of person can change the world? Write a draft of your post for the Unit 7 Review Discussion Point.

 "The people who are crazy enough to think they can change the world are the ones who do."
—Apple computer Inc. TV ad, 1997, selected from *Oxford Dictionary of American Quotations*,
2nd ed., edited by Hugh Rawson and Margaret Miner

11 Use the rubric from Exercise 9 to score your post. Then improve your post.

 Go online to add your comments to the discussion board.

8 Stories

Must and *must not / can't* ▸8.1

1 Choose the correct answers.

1 I _____ forget to do my homework tonight!

   a must   b must not

2 Do we _____ write 20 pages?

   a must   b have to

3 This story is so good! You _____ read it!

   a must   b can't

4 Every good story _____ have a good title. The title gets people's attention.

   a must   b must not

2 Choose the correct phrases to complete the paragraph from a university website.

You ¹*must not / must* follow rules when writing quotes. First, use quotation marks around the words. Quotation marks show that someone else said or wrote the idea. You ²*have to / can't* copy words without using quotation marks around them. Second, when writing a quote, the words must be the same. You ³*can't / must* change the words that someone else said or wrote. Third, you ⁴*must / must not* include the writer's name after the quote. People ⁵*have to / must* know the person's name.

Past continuous ▸8.2

3 Choose the correct words to complete the conversation.

A: There was an accident.

B: What happened?

A: Two friends ¹*was / were* hiking and got lost. They ²*was / were* arguing about the way to get back.

B: Then what happened?

A: One fell down a hill. He ³*was / were* yelling in pain. People heard him. They ⁴*was / were* searching for him when they found the other friend.

B: Wow! I'm glad people found them. Were they OK?

A: Well, the friend's leg was hurt, but after a while, he ⁵*was / were* walking again.

4 Correct the incorrect sentences.

1 When the fire started, I wasn't sleeping.

   _____

2 My son were sleeping in his room.

   _____

3 My neighbors was cooking late at night.

   _____

4 The stove weren't working.

   _____

Simple past and past continuous ▸8.3

5 Use the correct verb to complete each sentence.

1 I _____ cookies when I heard the scream!

   baked / was baking

2 The girl was swimming when the storm _____.

   began / was beginning

3 The boy wasn't looking at her when he _____ the promise.

   made / was making

4 She got very sick when she _____ in New York.

   traveled / was traveling

6 Complete the article with the verbs in the box. Use each verb once.

Simple Past	Past Continuous
walked stopped yelled	were walking was coming was talking

Son Saves Mom

Kyle and his mom ¹_____ to school. At a stop sign, a bus ²_____ to let people off. Kyle and his mom ³_____ into the street to cross, but another car ⁴_____. The driver ⁵_____ on the phone and didn't see the stop sign. Kyle ⁶_____ for his mom to stop. Kyle's mom was glad Kyle saw the car.

Verbs ▶8.1

1 Unscramble the verbs.

1 ocefr _____
2 geaur _____
3 oiadv _____
4 tgifh _____
5 thi _____
6 kema _____

2 Complete the sentences with a verb from Exercise 1.

1 Please keep your hands to yourself. Do not touch or _____ people next to you.

2 I can't _____ you to do your homework, but it's not possible to pass the class without doing it.

3 Do you talk to people when you are upset, or do you _____ them?

4 I don't _____ a promise I can't keep. I am an honest person.

Verbs ▶8.2

3 Look at the pictures. Then complete the verbs in the story titles. Write them in the simple past.

1 Kids Pr_____ to Be Firefighter and Police and Helped

2 New Helmet Pr_____ Biker

3 People E_____ Fire

4 Man Su_____ Accident

5 Police Se_____ the Woods

6 Boy Sa_____

4 Use the verbs in the box to replace the **bold** words.

escaped	~~pretended~~	protect	survived

1 Sadie **acted like** she was a teacher. She loved to play school. _____pretended_____

2 They **got out** from the car after it rolled down the hill. _____

3 She put her baby in the car seat in the back **to look after** her. _____

4 Their mother was in the hospital, but she **lived** after she fell through the ice. _____

VOCABULARY DEVELOPMENT:
Time expressions in stories ▶8.3

5 Are the time expressions in the correct place? Choose *Yes* or *No*.

	Yes	No
1 There was a kitten to his surprise in his car.	☐	☐
2 Immediately, the fire alarm went off.	☐	☐
3 Suddenly, people were running.	☐	☐
4 She eventually got out of her car.	☐	☐
5 The noise all of a sudden got louder.	☐	☐

6 For each pair, write *S* (similar) or *D* (different).

____ 1 all of a sudden / eventually

____ 2 immediately / to my surprise

____ 3 recently / suddenly

____ 4 suddenly / immediately

7 Choose the correct answers.

1 When I heard the crash, I _____ looked out the window.
a immediately   b recently

2 It was sunny a minute ago. Then _____ the sky turned black, and the sun went away.
a all of a sudden   b eventually

3 It _____ snowed, and now the roads are unsafe.
a eventually   b recently

4 The girl was searching for water. Hours later she _____ found some.
a eventually   b to my surprise

READING SKILL: Recognizing and understanding references:
Subject and object pronouns ▶8.2

1 Read the sentences. Write the noun or nouns the pronoun refers to.

1 The boy and girl were playing with a balloon when **it** popped. _____

2 The kids were lost in the woods, and the police could not find **them**. _____

3 The girl took her doll everywhere with **her**. _____

4 The mother called to her daughter, but her daugher did not hear **her**. _____

5 The brother and sister were having fun. **They** were pretending to be lifeguards.

   _____

2 Find the sentences in the text, and choose the noun the pronoun refers to.

1 **She** called to them.
   a girl   b mother   c brother
2 She called to **them**.
   a girl and doll   b mother and daughter c girl and brother
3 **We** aren't fighting.
   a girl and brother b girl and doll   c brother
4 Aaron saved **her**.
   a girl and doll   b girl   c doll
5 As **they** create stories, they think about people's feelings.
   a girl and brother b mother and daughter c children

READING: Practice

3 Read the article. When you were a child, what stories did you create?

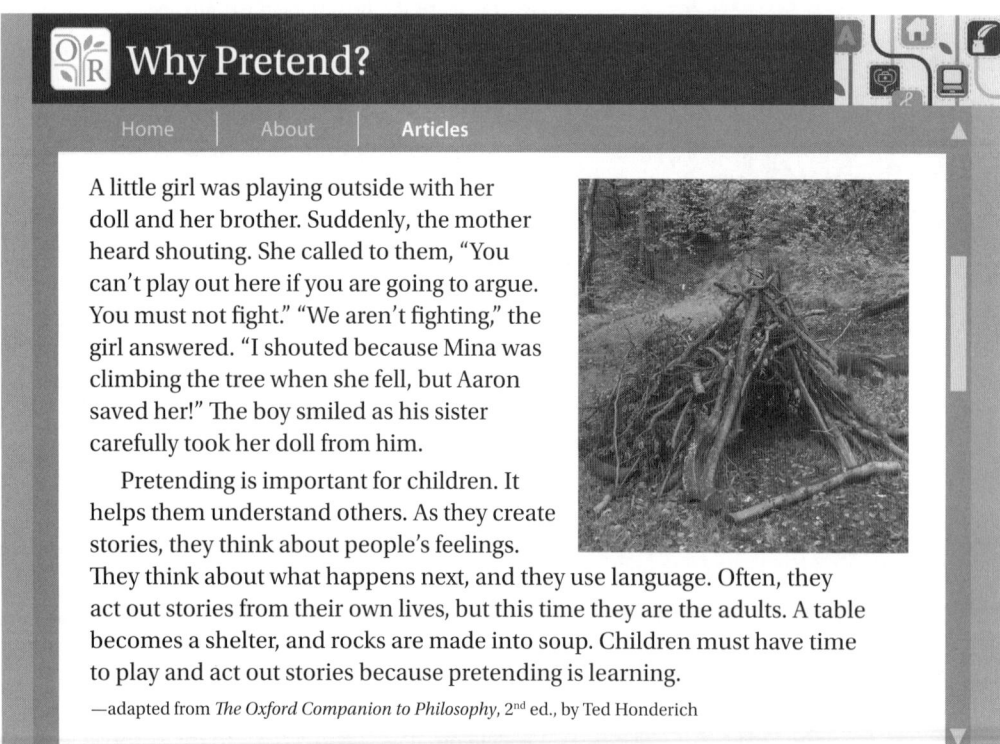

Why Pretend?

Home | About | **Articles**

A little girl was playing outside with her doll and her brother. Suddenly, the mother heard shouting. She called to them, "You can't play out here if you are going to argue. You must not fight." "We aren't fighting," the girl answered. "I shouted because Mina was climbing the tree when she fell, but Aaron saved her!" The boy smiled as his sister carefully took her doll from him.

Pretending is important for children. It helps them understand others. As they create stories, they think about people's feelings. They think about what happens next, and they use language. Often, they act out stories from their own lives, but this time they are the adults. A table becomes a shelter, and rocks are made into soup. Children must have time to play and act out stories because pretending is learning.

—adapted from *The Oxford Companion to Philosophy*, 2nd ed., by Ted Honderich

4 Write *T* (True) or *F* (False).

‗‗‗ 1 The girl fell out of the tree.

‗‗‗ 2 The boy and the girl were arguing.

‗‗‗ 3 The mother was angry with the children.

‗‗‗ 4 The boy and the girl were pretending.

‗‗‗ 5 The girl was happy with her brother.

‗‗‗ 6 The girl's name is Mina.

‗‗‗ 7 The boy saved the doll.

5 Number the events in the correct order. The first and last are numberd for you.

‗‗‗ The mother heard shouting.

‗‗‗ The girl said they weren't fighting.

_5_ The boy smiled and gave the doll back.

_1_ The girl was playing with her doll and her brother.

‗‗‗ The mother told the children not to fight.

6 What do you think the writer agrees with? Choose *Agree* or *Disagree*.

	Agree	Disagree
1 Pretending helps children understand other people.	☐	☐
2 Children should not make up stories.	☐	☐
3 Pretending is good for developing language.	☐	☐
4 Children need more time for pretend play.	☐	☐
5 Adults may not understand the importance of pretending.	☐	☐
6 It's not good for children to pretend to be adults.	☐	☐
7 Going to school is more important than acting out stories.	☐	☐

REAL-WORLD ENGLISH: Showing interest ▶8.4

1 @ Watch the video. Match the response with another that has a similar meaning.

_____ 1 Of course! Andy!   a Oh? Really?

_____ 2 I see.   b Right! How are you?

_____ 3 Is that right?   c Actually

_____ 4 That's amazing!   d Right.

_____ 5 As a matter of fact   e Wow!

2 Read the conversations. Choose *1* (some interest), *3* (stronger interest), or *5* (very strong interest) to describe the response.

		1	3	5
1	A: Hey, we are in Calculus together! On Tuesdays?			
	B: Right...	☐	☐	☐
2	A: I'm going to be in your lab group!			
	B: Cool.	☐	☐	☐
3	A: I traveled through Egypt last year.			
	B: Really? Wow!	☐	☐	☐
4	A: I was working on a research project.			
	B: Oh? Is that right?	☐	☐	☐
5	A: I was studying Arabic and interviewing people. It was awesome.			
	B: That sounds amazing!	☐	☐	☐

3 Write a response from the box to show a little (–) or a lot of (+) interest.

Oh? What's wrong with it?	Right. You're Dan.	Really? That's interesting.
Oh no! Are you OK?	I see.	

1 We met last night when the study group was taking a break. –

_____

2 I'm a writer. +

_____

3 Jen is my manager. –

_____

4 I'm not that happy with my job. +

_____

5 I was in a bike accident yesterday. +

_____

1 🔊 Listen to the Unit Review Podcast. What is the purpose of this news? You can choose more than one answer.

1 to persuade ☐
2 to inform ☐
3 to entertain ☐

UNIT REVIEW: Podcast

📲 **Go online to listen to the podcast from the Unit Review.**

2 🔊 Listen to the Unit Review Podcast. Are the sentences correct? Choose *Yes* or *No*.

	Yes	No
1 Sita Patel is a news writer.	☐	☐
2 More people read an article about a new baby in the royal family than a horse in McDonald's.	☐	☐
3 McDonald's told the woman to come in with her horse.	☐	☐
4 If you want readers, you should put an animal name in your new story title.	☐	☐

3 🔊 Listen again. Complete the sentences with the word you hear.

1 What stories get the most **c**_____?

2 A woman was riding her horse when she **d**_____ to get some food.

3 McDonald's would not serve her. She **a**_____.

4 Wow, well, I guess that is interesting, but so is a new baby in the royal **f**_____.

5 "Man **e**_____ fire with a kitten." That's news!

DISCUSSION BOARD PREPARATION

4 Look at the Unit 8 Review Discussion Point. Read the questions in the prompt. Then read the reply. Label the part of the reply that answers the question.

5 What type of news does the student think is interesting?

_____

_____

6 Why does the student think that news is interesting?

_____

_____

7 Do you think the student agrees with the news writer from the Unit Podcast about what is interesting? Why or why not?

_____

Unit 8 Review Discussion Point

Read the quote. What kind of news do you think is interesting?
"When a dog bites a man, that is not news. But when a man bites a dog, that is news."
—Charles Dana (American journalist), selected from *Oxford Dictionary of American Quotations*,
2nd ed., edited by Hugh Rawson and Margaret Miner

Latest: Nazar Uksander
one hour ago
I like news stories about crazy things that happen. It's always interesting when someone is saved or survives an accident. The details can be so scary. If there is a good ending, I feel happy. But I feel very bad if it isn't good so me read other stories too. I read news about my country. I want to know what happens there. I don't live there now, but I did, so I am interested in it.
    I think the most interesting news is something from my country or about a problem, like a fire that people escape. When I read about a problem, I want to know how it ends. I want to understand the details and imagine it. I pretend I am there. It's the same for news from my country. I can imagine it. I can feel like I'm there.

8 Overall, did the writer answer the question? If yes, explain. If no, what can the writer change?

_____

_____

9 Review the rubric. Use the rubric to give a score for the reply.
Give points: 0 (not successful)–10 (successful).

Writing a Discussion Board Post	Points
The writer answers the question in the prompt.	
The writer explains his or her ideas.	
The writer organizes ideas.	
The writer uses subject and object pronouns correctly.	
The writer uses unit vocabulary correctly.	
The post is long enough (100–150 words).	
Total	

WRITE YOUR POST

10 Read the quote. What kind of news do you think is interesting? Write a draft of your post for the Unit 8 Review Discussion Point.

"When a dog bites a man, that is not news. But when a man bites a dog, that is news."
—Charles Dana (American journalist), selected from *Oxford Dictionary of American Quotations*, 2nd ed., edited by Hugh Rawson and Margaret Miner

11 Use the rubric from Exercise 9 to score your post. Then improve your post.

 Go online to add your comments to the discussion board.

9 Future

Going to and will for predictions ▶9.1

1 Correct the mistakes in *going to* and *will* for predictions.

1 In the future, food will very different from today.

_____

2 Some people is going to grow their own food.

_____

3 There are going to be less clean water to drink.

_____

4 More people live in big cities. _____

5 Most people going to live alone. _____

2 Complete the conversations with the correct form of *going to* and *will*.

1 A: In 2050, _____ people drive cars?

   B: No, they _____.

2 A: Are people _____ to have jobs?

   B: Yes, they _____. People will work with robots.

3 A: Will there _____ libraries?

   B: No, there _____.

4 A: _____ people going to be happier?

   B: I don't know, but they _____ live longer.

Be going to and will for future plans and decisions ▶9.2

3 Make questions using *be going to* and *will*. Then answer the questions about you.

1 going / where / to / you / are / work

_____?

_____.

2 will / you / live / where

_____?

_____.

3 to / what / going / are / do in the summer / you

_____?

_____.

4 Write questions about the **bold** words in the answers.

1 A: _Who is he going to marry?_

   B: He's going to marry my best friend **Gloria**.

2 A: _____

   B: I'm going to travel **to Lebanon**.

3 A: _____

   B: I'll work in Mexico **next summer**.

4 A: _____

   B: He's going out to dinner **for his birthday**.

5 A: _____

   B: No, I won't **tell you my business idea**.

A / an, the, and no article ▶9.3

5 Are the sentences correct? Choose *Yes* or *No*.

	Yes	No
1 Are you going to be the musician?	☐	☐
2 Will you buy a electric car?	☐	☐
3 Is that the science building?	☐	☐
4 That's a great idea!	☐	☐
5 Do you know where the lab is?	☐	☐

6 Read the job description. Complete the sentences with *a / an*, *the*, or – (nothing).

Teacher Needed

We are looking for [1]_____ English teacher with three years of experience. The teacher will teach [2]_____ four online classes each semester. [3]_____ classes will be taught in [4]_____ online classroom. Each class will have [5]_____ 10 to 15 students. [6]_____ students will be from all over the world. [7]_____ teacher must have experience with technology. He or she will need to have [8]_____ online office hours three times a week for two hours. He or she will create all tests and classroom coursework.

Computer Programmer Needed

We are looking for [9]_____ computer programmer. [10]_____ programmer will manage 200 robots. [11]_____ robots build and repair hospital equipment. He or she will work on [12]_____ team with three other computer programmers.

Verbs for prediction ▶9.1

1 Use a word from the box to describe the comments.

| expects | imagine | predicted | worries |

1 "I get very upset about the future. There will be too many people and not enough jobs." She _____ about the future.

2 "I love walking in the woods. I can't think of a better place to relax and enjoy the world." She can't _____ a better place.

3 "I think doctors will always be humans and not robots. I don't want robots caring for me." In the future, he _____ that doctors will be humans.

4 "The weather forecast is bad today. There will be ice and snow." The forecast _____ ice and snow.

2 Do you agree or disagree? Write *A* or *D*.

1 I **guess** that schools will not have computer labs in the future. ____

2 I **imagine** that in the future people will be nicer to each other. ____

3 I **expect** that in the future everyone will design and make their own clothes with machines. ____

4 I **worry** that the sea levels are becoming dangerous for people on islands. ____

5 I **believe** everyone in the future will use driverless cars. ____

3 Choose all the answers that complete the sentence.

1 I _____ that there will be bad traffic.
   ☐ worry   ☐ predict
   ☐ imagine   ☐ expect

2 I can't _____ a better place than Earth.
   ☐ guess   ☐ believe
   ☐ imagine   ☐ expect

3 I _____ we will be OK.
   ☐ worry   ☐ believe
   ☐ imagine   ☐ expect

VOCABULARY DEVELOPMENT: Future time expressions ▶9.2

4 Unscramble the words to complete the sentences with time expressions.

1 I will visit Bolivia in a N M T H O! _____

2 I will take a vacation after A U G T R D O I A N. _____

3 We are going to a music concert next E E E W N D K. _____

4 I will be in the United Kingdom for the next few E R Y A S. _____

5 Bye! I'll see you the day after R O W T M R O O! _____

5 Match the question in A with the answer in B.

A

1 Where will you live after graduation? ____

2 When will you graduate? ____

3 When will you go to Peru? ____

4 Where will you be in the future? ____

B

a Next semester. I'm going with my whole class.

b By age 35, I'll be a teacher in Japan.

c Next June, I'll move downtown. I'll be closer to my new job.

d I won't finish school for a while. This is my first year.

6 Answer the questions using the words in parentheses.

1 When will they visit New York? (in a month)
   _____

2 When are you going to study? (soon)
   _____

3 When will Josh start his new job? (next summer)
   _____

4 When will Lynn's parents visit? (next weekend)
   _____

5 When are you going to graduate? (by age 22)
   _____

1 Read the letter to the editor and the reply. What do you predict for the student's future?

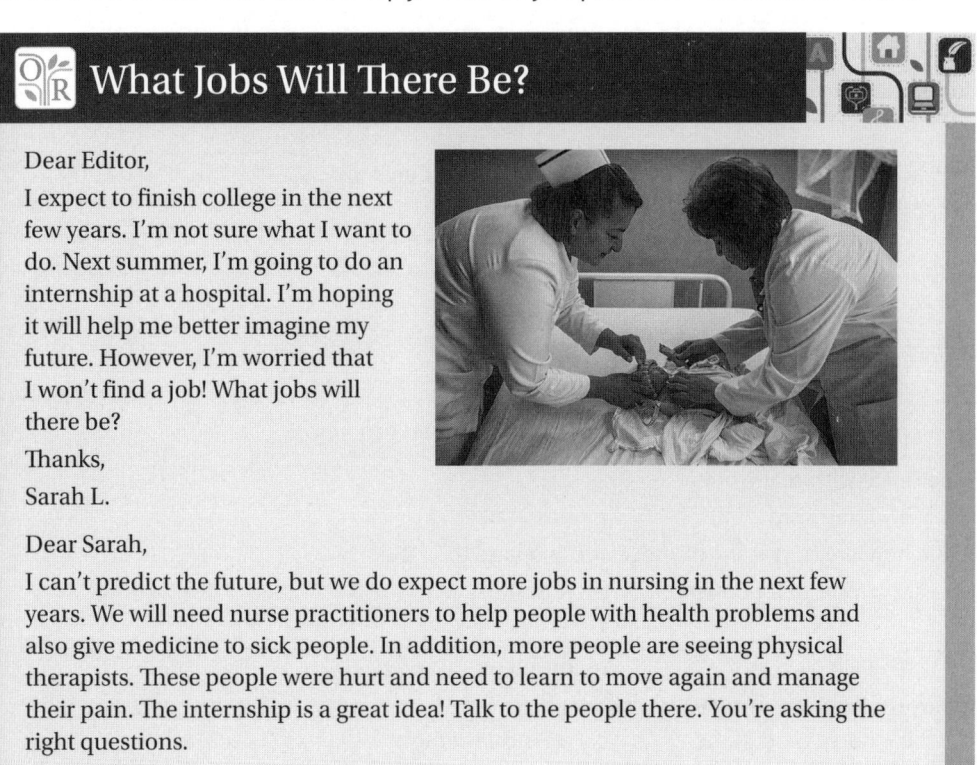

What Jobs Will There Be?

Dear Editor,

I expect to finish college in the next few years. I'm not sure what I want to do. Next summer, I'm going to do an internship at a hospital. I'm hoping it will help me better imagine my future. However, I'm worried that I won't find a job! What jobs will there be?

Thanks,

Sarah L.

Dear Sarah,

I can't predict the future, but we do expect more jobs in nursing in the next few years. We will need nurse practitioners to help people with health problems and also give medicine to sick people. In addition, more people are seeing physical therapists. These people were hurt and need to learn to move again and manage their pain. The internship is a great idea! Talk to the people there. You're asking the right questions.

All the best!

Colin Anderson

—adapted from *A Dictionary of Nursing*, 7th ed., by Elizabeth A. Martin and Tanya A. McFerran and *A Dictionary of Public Health*, edited by John M. Last

2 Match the questions with the correct responses.

Does the student know what she wants to do?
Will the student have an internship?
Will there be jobs in nursing?
Will the editor predict the future?
Does the editor say there will be jobs in business management?

1 _____

Yes, she will.

2 _____

Yes, there will.

3 _____

No, he won't.

4 _____

No, she doesn't.

5 _____

No, he doesn't.

3 Who shares these things? Choose *Sarah, Colin,* or *No One.*

	Sarah	Colin	No One
1 There will be jobs in nursing in the future.	☐	☐	☐
2 The internship will help to imagine the future.	☐	☐	☐
3 I can't predict the future.	☐	☐	☐
4 I'm worried about the future.	☐	☐	☐
5 There won't be jobs.	☐	☐	☐
6 There will be jobs for doctors.	☐	☐	☐
7 Talk to the people at the internship.	☐	☐	☐
8 Finish college by 2025.	☐	☐	☐

READING SKILL: Using context clues ▶9.1

4 Choose the correct word to match the definition. Use context clues from the text to help.

1 A job to give a student experience with real work
  a nurse practictioner   b internship   c hospital

2 A person who helps people who were hurt learn to move and manage their pain
  a physical therapist   b nurse practitioner   c hospital

3 A bad feeling in your body
  a medicine   b pain   c problem

4 A person who helps people with health problems and sick people
  a medicine   b nurse practitioner   c physical therapist

5 The liquid or pills you take to feel better
  a pain   b sick   c medicine

5 Find the context clues that tell the meaning of the word in **bold**.

1 There is going to be a need for **computer programmers**. Many businesses will need people to create directions for their computers.

2 There will also be a need for **financial advisers**. Many people need others to help them manage their money.

3 We won't need as many **telemarketers**. Computers will be able to make phone calls and give information about things for sale.

4 Many more people will be **self-employed**. It's better to work for yourself.

5 There is going to be a lot more **recycling**. People want to use their things again instead of throwing them away.

1 🔊 Watch the video. Complete the dialogue from Scene 1 of the video with words from the box.

| amazing | nervous | nice | OK | sure | worry | really |

Dave: Hello, Andy.

Andy: ¹_____ work.

Dave: Huh?

Andy: Yeah. It looks ²_____!

Dave: ³_____? Thank you.

Andy: Are you ⁴_____? You seem … ⁵_____.

Dave: Well … the exhibit does begin in 15 minutes. Where is everyone?

Andy: Don't ⁶_____. A lot of people are coming to your show.

Dave: Are you ⁷_____?

2 🔊 Listen for the comments in the video. Match the comments to the descriptions.

| upset | expressing doubt | nervous | encouraging | very encouraging |

1   Where is everyone? _____

2   Don't worry. _____

3   Are you sure? _____

4   You always do well, Dave. There's nothing to worry about. _____

5   Huh? Right! _____

3 Does the phrase show doubt or encouragement?

	Doubt	Encouragement
1 Everything's going to be fine.	☐	☐
2 Do you really think so?	☐	☐
3 I'm not sure.	☐	☐
4 You did really well!	☐	☐
5 Really?	☐	☐
6 Don't worry.	☐	☐

4 Read the conversation. Answer the questions.

Colleague 1:   So, how is your first week going?

Colleague 2:   It's OK….I'm trying to be positive, but I'm not sure I'm doing everything right.

Colleague 1:   Oh.

1   The new colleague *worries / feels good* about her work.

2   The other colleague *shows / does not show* encouragement.

3   The new colleague *shows / does not show* doubt.

LISTENING SKILL: Focusing on key words ▶9.3

1 🔊 Listen. Complete the sentences with the key words you hear.

1 Hank, the big _____ is the _____ after _____.

2 Did you ever _____ you would be _____ against a _____?

3 _____, if you told me this _____ ago, I would _____ have _____ you.

4 And do you _____ about the _____?

5 Are _____ still going to be _____ in the next _____ or _____?

UNIT REVIEW: Podcast

@ **Go online to listen to the podcast from the Unit Review.**

2 🔊 Listen to the Unit Review Podcast. Choose the correct words.

1 Hank's job is a *cab driver / race car driver*.

2 The race is between Hank and a *famous driver / driverless car*.

3 Hank *expects / does not expect* to have his job in the future.

4 Hank *thinks / does not think* robots will entertain us in the future.

5 Hank *expected / did not expect* this race to happen.

6 Hank has had his job for *ten / twenty* years.

7 Hank *predicts / does not predict* he will win.

3 🔊 Listen again. Match the words to make a phrase from the podcast.

expect	future	happen	so	still

1 are you _____ going to be

2 worry about the _____

3 I believe _____

4 predict what is going to _____

5 who do you _____ to win the big race

DISCUSSION BOARD PREPARATION

4 Look at the Unit 9 Review Discussion Point. Read the questions in the prompt. Then read the reply. Label the part of the reply that answers question 1. Label the part that answers question 2.

5 Who does the writer think helped invent the future?

_____

6 How does the writer explain how the person invented the future?

_____

7 What idea does the writer have for an invention, and how did he get the idea?

_____

Unit 9 Review Discussion Point

1 Read the quote and discuss these questions: Can you think of someone who helped to invent the future? How did they do it?

"The best way to predict the future is to invent it."

—Ian Kay (American computer scientist), in *Oxford Essential Quotations*, 5th ed., edited by Susan Ratcliffe

2 What ideas do you have for inventions for the future?

Latest: Yuan Li
one hour ago
Mark Zuckerberg is a good example. He helped to invent the future. He was in college, and he saw that people wanted to talk to each other more easily. He created Facebook, so people could have a group online and share information. He wanted to use it, and he knew his friends did, too.

I have an idea for an invention. By 2030, I predict that people won't go grocery shopping. I believe people will buy all their food online, so I have an idea for how to use all the empty grocery store buildings. I am going to create a new business for an adventure gym. It's a place people can go to climb, skateboard, and do extreme sports. It will be fun! I predict it will be successful because there are many new gyms in my city. I like to do sports, so I think others will like the idea too.

8 Overall, did the writer answer all the questions? If yes, explain. If no, what can the writer change?

_____

_____

9 Review the rubric. Use the rubric to give a score for the reply.
Give points: 0 (not successful)–10 (successful).

Writing a Discussion Board Post	Points
The writer gives an example of someone who helped invent the future.	
The writer explains ideas for inventions for the future.	
The writer uses *going to* and *will* for predictions.	
The writer uses articles correctly.	
The writer uses future time expressions correctly.	
The post is long enough (100–150 words).	
Total	

WRITE YOUR POST

10 Read the quote and discuss these questions: Can you think of someone who helped to invent the future? How did they do it? Write a draft of your post for the Unit 9 Review Discussion Point.

"The best way to predict the future is to invent it."

—Alan Kay (American computer scientist), in *Oxford Essential Quotations*, 5th ed., edited by Susan Ratcliffe

11 Use the rubric from Exercise 9 to score your post. Then improve your post.

Go online to add your comments to the discussion board.

10 Performance

-ing forms ▶10.1

1 Find eight -ing forms that are used as nouns.

A: Did you know studying music is good for the brain?

B: Yes, I've heard that. Reading music can improve your math skills, right?

A: Yeah, but it's not just reading music that is good. Learning rhythm is important.

C: Wow, that's so cool. So listening to music is helpful?

A: Yeah. Recognizing the patterns in music is connected to math skills.

B: Ha! Well, I did do a lot of clapping and singing in school. Maybe that's why I'm so good at math!

2 Choose the correct word to complete each sentence.

1 _____ another language is good for people.

Learn / Learning

2 I like to _____ guitar.

play / playing

3 My brother is good at _____.

run / running

4 I _____ theater to college students.

teach / teaching

Review of comparative and superlative adjectives; comparative adverbs ▶10.2

3 Complete the sentences with the correct form.

Comparative and superlative adjectives

1 Computers are _____ than they were 20 years ago. (small)

2 The _____ person today is over 8 feet tall. (tall)

3 The _____ person today is 22 inches tall. (short)

Comparative adverbs

4 We can prepare meals _____ today than in the past. (fast)

5 I eat vegetables _____ now. (regularly)

6 We eat _____ than we did in the past. (well)

4 Correct the incorrect sentences.

1 Running shoes are light than they were 20 years ago.

_____

2 Caffeine can help you run faster.

_____

3 A cup of coffee is the better drink to have before a race.

_____

4 I run slowly after a big meal than a small snack.

_____

Comparative adjectives: *(not) as...as*; negative comparatives and superlatives: *Less* and *least* ▶10.3

5 Complete the sentences with the missing word to make comparatives and superlatives.

1 Going to a concert is _____ exciting than seeing a dance performance. I love dance!

2 Listening to music at home is just as nice _____ hearing it at a concert.

3 A fashion show is the _____ interesting show to see. Nothing really happens!

4 Watching a movie at home is _____ as fun as seeing one in the theater. I like being part of a crowd.

5 Reading a book is just _____ entertaining as seeing the movie. I love to imagine the characters.

6 Write a sentence to compare the two things. Use the words in parentheses and the correct form of *be*.

1 Child actors / adult actors (just as successful)

Child actors are just as successful as adult actors.

2 Sports equipment from 100 years ago / sports equipment now (less helpful)

_____

3 Watching a race on TV / seeing a race in person (not as exciting)

_____

4 Theater actors / movie actors (less famous)

_____

VOCABULARY DEVELOPMENT:
Adjective + preposition ▶10.1

1 Match the the beginning of the sentence in A with the ending in B.

A

1   I don't like talking in front of a lot of people. I am scared ____

2   I am a teacher. I am responsible ____

3   I am a musician. I am good ____

4   I don't like dance classes. I am nervous ____

5   I love to read about history. I am interested ____

6   I am not a student. I am different ____

B

a   about following directions and moving correctly.

b   for creating lessons and grading work.

c   of speaking to a big group.

d   in world events and the past.

e   at playing the piano.

f   from my friends at the university.

2 Match a word in A to a word in B and complete the sentences below.

A

interested	nervous	necessary
successful	proud	different

B

from	of	at	for	about	in

1   People all over the world listen to our podcasts.

We are _____ making interesting shows.

2   I like to read about ways to stay calm.

I'm _____ learning to relax.

3   I do not like to talk at work meetings.

I'm _____ my performance in front of others.

4   I gave a great dance performance tonight!

I'm _____ my hard work and practice.

5   I am very good at presenting. Other people get

nervous, but not me. I'm _____ them.

6   I am a professional athlete. I run 60 miles a week. The

practice time is _____ my performance.

Performers and performances ▶10.3

3 Read the text. Number the pictures in the order from the text.

The Top Five Performance Careers

First is being an award-winning [1]**movie star**. Many people want to be rich and famous. Next is being a [2]**famous musician**. Many people think playing a concert in front of millions sounds exciting. Number three on the list is being a [3]**model**. Who doesn't want to be beautiful? After that, people want to [4]**act on a stage** in theater. Last is being a [5]**dancer**. This takes a lot of skill and practice.

4 Choose the correct answers.

1   What do you call someone who plays an instrument such as the piano?
    a   a musician   b   a dancer
    c   a model

2   What do you call an event that is happening now in front of you?
    a   a stage   b   a live performance
    c   a fashion show

3   What do you call the place where an actor performs?
    a   a stage   b   a show
    c   a concert

4   What do you call a person who shows clothing in a fashion show?
    a   a star   b   a model
    c   a dancer

5   What do you call a famous person in movies?
    a   a movie star   b   a fashion model
    c   a stage actor

READING SKILL: Previewing ▶10.2

1 Look at the picture, and read the title. What question will the text answer?

a Why do people perform? ☐

b What do people like to perform? ☐

c How can you prepare to perform? ☐

d What are the best performances? ☐

e How should you feel when you perform? ☐

2 Read the first and last sentences of the text. Choose the main idea.

a Being nervous is not OK. ☐

b There are ways to feel better before a performance. ☐

c Many people get sick at a performance. ☐

d Going to performances can make people nervous. ☐

e Anxiety is bad for your heart. ☐

READING: Practice

3 Read the article. What things do you already do?

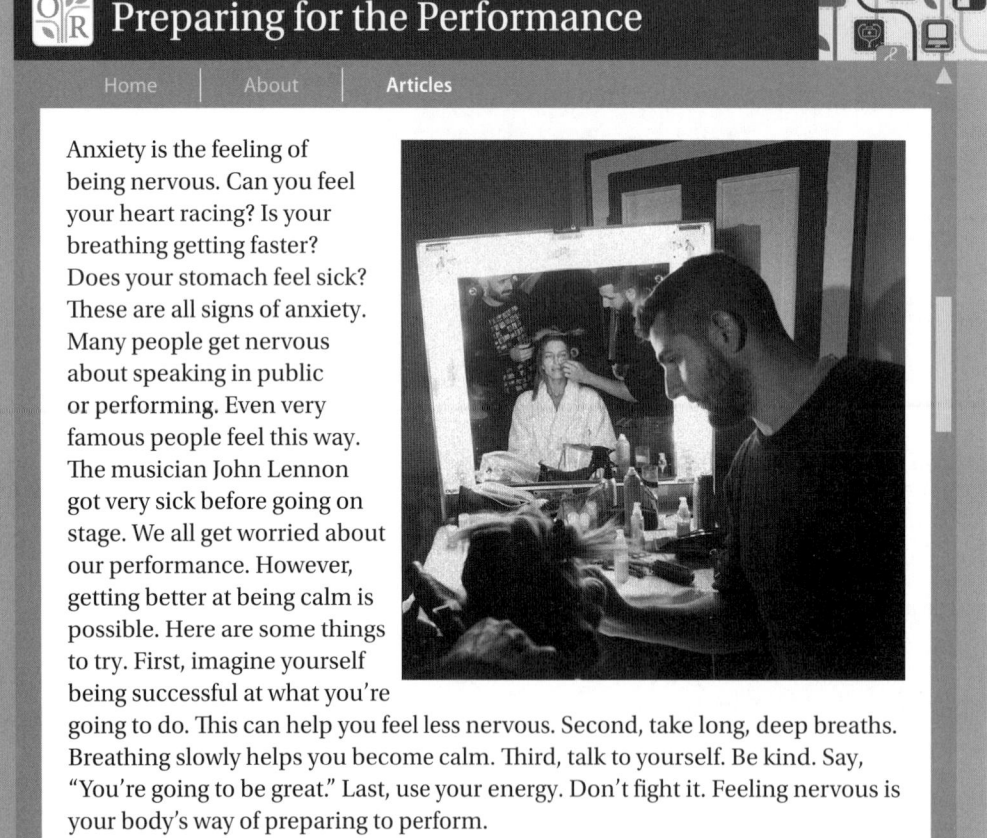

Preparing for the Performance

Home | About | **Articles**

Anxiety is the feeling of being nervous. Can you feel your heart racing? Is your breathing getting faster? Does your stomach feel sick? These are all signs of anxiety. Many people get nervous about speaking in public or performing. Even very famous people feel this way. The musician John Lennon got very sick before going on stage. We all get worried about our performance. However, getting better at being calm is possible. Here are some things to try. First, imagine yourself being successful at what you're going to do. This can help you feel less nervous. Second, take long, deep breaths. Breathing slowly helps you become calm. Third, talk to yourself. Be kind. Say, "You're going to be great." Last, use your energy. Don't fight it. Feeling nervous is your body's way of preparing to perform.

—adapted from *A Dictionary of Sports Studies* by Alan Tomlinson

4 Are these signs of anxiety? Choose *Yes* or *No*.

		Yes	No
1	long, deep breaths	☐	☐
2	racing heart	☐	☐
3	stomach feels sick	☐	☐
4	breathing faster	☐	☐
5	becoming calm	☐	☐

5 Complete the sentences with words from the reading.

1 Think of yourself being _____ at your performance.

2 Breathe _____ to become calm.

3 Say nice things to _____.

4 Use your energy. Don't _____ your feelings.

5 Your body is getting ready for the _____.

6 Match the questions to the answers.

_____ 1 What famous musician got sick before performing?

_____ 2 What does feeling nervous help you do?

_____ 3 Who should you say kind things to?

_____ 4 What does breathing slowly help you do?

_____ 5 Who gets nervous before performing?

a many people

b John Lennon

c become calm

d yourself

e prepare to perform

REAL-WORLD ENGLISH: Accepting / refusing invitations ▶10.4

1 Match the questions with the responses from the video.

____ 1 Hey, Max! What's going on?

____ 2 Are you busy tomorrow afternoon?

____ 3 So … would you like to come?

____ 4 Are you busy in the afternoon? Do you want to come?

____ 5 You can't? Erm.

a Tomorrow? Erm, no, I don't think I'm busy. Why?

b Sorry, Kevin. I can't make it.

c But thanks for inviting me.

d Hey, Kev. Uh … I'm on my way to the library.

e Tennis? Sure! That sounds good!

2 Match each speaker from the video with the correct action.

____ Max

____ Andy

____ Kevin

a gives an invitation

b accepts an invitation

c refuses the invitation

3 Complete the conversation with the correct words to invite, refuse, and accept invitations.

1 A: Hey, Sara! Are you doing anything tonight?

   B: No, _____?

   A: I'm going to my professor's art show? Do you want to come?

   B: Sure! I'd love _____.

2 A: Are you _____ tomorrow?

   B: Well, I have swim practice. Why do you _____?

   A: Oh, OK, I was going to invite you to my sister's dance show, but it's a far drive.

   B: That's _____ bad. It sounds fun. Maybe another time?

3 A: Are you busy right now?

   B: Right now? _____ really.

   A: I'm going to my professor's art show. Want to come?

   B: Oh, _____ for asking, but I have to do homework for class tomorrow. Have fun.

4 A: Hi, Khalid, it's so nice to see you again. I was hoping to run into you.

   B: Really?

   A: Yeah, I was wondering … Would you like to come to dinner with a couple of friends and me tomorrow?

   B: That sounds great. I'd love to. Thanks _____ much for asking. What time?

4 Write *1*, *2*, *3*, or *4* to match the conversations from Exercise 3 to the correct statements.

____ ____ 1 The invitation is accepted.

____ ____ 2 The invitation is refused.

____ 3 The responder says he is not busy.

____ 4 The responder is sorry to miss the event.

____ 5 The responder thanks the person for the invitation.

____ 6 The invitation is formal.

LISTENING SKILL: Listening for gist ▶10.1

1 🔊 Listen to the Unit Review Podcast. Choose five important content phrases you hear.

- ☐ fashion adviser
- ☐ look their best
- ☐ explain your job
- ☐ part of it
- ☐ more interested
- ☐ wearing the right clothes
- ☐ big events
- ☐ feel successful
- ☐ dressed for success

2 🔊 Listen again. Look at your words from Exercise 1. Choose the main idea.

a   Fashion advisers have the best jobs.   ☐

b   Wear the right clothes to feel successful.   ☐

c   Look your best at a job interview.   ☐

d   Wear the right clothes to big events.   ☐

UNIT REVIEW: Podcast

🔊 **Go online to listen to the podcast from the Unit Review.**

3 🔊 Listen to the Unit Review Podcast again, and choose the correct words.

1   Tom's main point is your clothes can help you feel *better / worse*.

2   *Many / Not many* people are worried about their daily work.

3   Tom thinks we are *often / not often* performing.

4   People are *just as / not as* worried about small events as big events.

5   Tom is interested in how people *feel / do*.

4 🔊 Listen again and complete the conversation.

A: What are the "right" clothes? Do you mean for job interviews or public speaking, like

being on ¹_____?

B: Well, ²_____, that's part of it. But I'm ³_____ in how people want to

⁴_____. People are ⁵_____ their daily work as they are big events.

DISCUSSION BOARD PREPARATION

5   Look at the Unit 10 Review Discussion Point. Read the questions in the prompt. Then read the reply. Label the sentence that tells if the writer agrees or disagrees.

_____

6   What does the writer think is not good?

_____

7   What example does the writer use to explain her thinking?

_____

Unit 10 Review Discussion Point

1   Read the quote. Is it better to promise less ("under promise") and do more than you promise ("over perform")?
    What example can you give to show this?
    "Under promise. Over perform."
    —Michael Eisner (chairman and CEO of the Walt Disney Company) in *Oxford Dictionary of American Quotations,*
    2nd ed., edited by Hugh Rawsom and Margaret Miner

Latest: Alana Ruiz
one hour ago
It's better to under promise and then over perform. Everyone is scared of performing, but it's worse when people expect a lot from you. Then they think you could be better, and even if you did well, you feel bad.
   I have an example from my life. I was good at school work, but it was necessary for me to study a lot. I had to work really hard. My teachers didn't know I had to work so hard. They thought school was easy for me. When I was not great at something, they thought I didn't try. I wish they didn't think I was so good. Then I would not feel bad. I could be proud of my work even if it wasn't perfect. It's better to under promise because then people are proud of you when you do better.

8 Look at the last sentence of the reply. What does it tell you?

_____

9 Do you think the student agrees with the fashion adviser from the Unit Review Podcast?
Why or why not?

_____

_____

10 Review the rubric. Use the rubric to give a score for the reply.
Give points: 0 (not successful)–10 (successful).

Writing a Discussion Board Post	Points
The post answers the questions clearly and completely.	
The post has an opening sentence and a closing sentence.	
The post has clear explanations and examples.	
The writer uses adjectives and prepositions correctly.	
Sentences are complete and have correct punctuation.	
The post is long enough (100–150 words).	
Total	

WRITE YOUR POST

11 Read the quote. Is it better to promise less ("under promise") and do more than you promise ("over perform")? What example can you give to show this?

"Under promise. Over perform."
—Michael Eisner (chairman and CEO of the Walt Disney Company) in *Oxford Dictionary of American Quotation*, 2nd ed., edited by Hugh Rawsom and Margaret Miner

12 Use the rubric from Exercise 10 to score your post. Then improve your post.

Go ONLINE to add your comments to the discussion board.

11 Experiences

Present perfect with *for* and *since* ▶11.1

1 Correct the mistakes in the present perfect with *for* and *since*.

1 I worked as a tour guide in Beijing, China, since 2012.

   _____have worked_____

2 My family have visited me each summer for two years.

   _____

3 We have study Chinese for six years! _____

4 The Great Wall of China attracted visitors to China for hundreds of years. _____

2 Write the words in the correct order to make sentences.

1 been / in Peru / since / I / last September. / have

   _____

2 I was five. / wanted to study / since / I have / in Peru

   _____

3 saved money / for my trip / I / over two years. / for / have

   _____

4 1911. / people / since / more interest in / have had / Machu Picchu

   _____

Present perfect with *just, already,* and *yet* ▶11.2

3 Are the sentences correct? Choose *Yes* or *No*.

	Yes	No
1 Have you been to South America just?	☐	☐
2 I've already visited five continents.	☐	☐
3 Have you see the Great Wall of China yet?	☐	☐
4 There have already been four car accidents on the road to Machu Picchu.	☐	☐
5 I haven't found yet the tour group.	☐	☐

4 Correct the incorrect sentences from Exercise 3.

1 _____

2 _____

3 _____

5 Write sentences with the words. Use the present perfect.

1 Kyoko / run / four marathons (already)

   _Kyoko has already run four marathons_____.

2 James and Hector / not go / on the tour (yet)

   _____

3 We / visit / Machu Picchu (just)

   _____

4 I / eat / at that famous restaurant (already)

   _____

5 you / be / to New York City (yet)

   _____?

Present perfect with *ever* and *never* ▶11.3

6 Match the question to the answers.

1 Have you ever swum with sharks? ____

2 Has Maria ever met anyone famous? ____

3 Have you or your friend ever mountain biked? ____

4 Have you ever been in an online video? ____

5 Has your teacher ever missed class? ____

a Yes, we have. It was a lot of fun.

b No, never! That sounds scary. Have you?

c Yes, I have once. I'm playing the piano in it.

d No, he hasn't. I guess he's never sick.

e Yes, she has. Once she met the president.

7 Complete the conversations with the missing words for present perfect with *ever* or *never*.

1 A: Have you _____ been rafting?

   B: No, I _____, but I want to.

2 A: _____ your family ever visited you here?

   B: Yes, they'_____ visited. They love it here!

3 A: Have you ever _____ to Korea?

   B: Yes, I _____. My grandparents live there.

4 A: _____ you ever parachuted from a plane?

   B: No, I _____! And I don't want to!

5 A: Have you _____ swum in freezing water?

   B: No, I _____ have, and I don't think I will!

VOCABULARY DEVELOPMENT: Collocations with *for* and *since* ▶11.1

1 Complete the sentences with the correct words for collocations with *for* and *since*.

1 Professors have taught classes at the University of Oxford _____ 1096.

2 I have wanted to go to the university since I _____ 14.

3 The University of Salamanca in Spain has also had students for hundreds _____ years.

4 Students have gone there _____ 1134.

5 Going to a university with a long past has been a dream of mine for _____ long time.

2 Choose the best answer.

1 I have been a student in France *for / since* two years.
2 I have studied French *for / since* high school.
3 I have lived with a French family *for / since* last summer.
4 They have lived in Paris *for / since* a long time.
5 I've also studied Arabic *for / since* a while.
6 I have wanted to live in France *since / for* I was 10!

3 Correct the incorrect sentences.

1 I have wanted to go whitewater rafting for a long time.

_____

2 My brother and I have lived in England since two years.

_____

3 I have planned to travel the world for I was 15!

_____

4 My mother has visited five different countries since last year!

_____

5 My brother has translated for my grandparents for he was young.

_____

6 I have been very happy with my life experiences and choices for a while now.

_____

Language learning ▶11.2

4 Choose the correct word to complete each sentence.

1 My _____ is to learn four new words a day.

  a progress   b translate   c goal

2 Using note cards is a simple but very good _____ for learning new words.

  a memory   b method   c meaning

3 Many words in English have more than one _____. For example, *pool* can be a verb or a noun.

  a progress   b method   c meaning

4 The Incan _____ was very interesting. The Incan people built Machu Picchu.

  a culture   b progress   c communicate

5 We've made a lot of _____ in the past ten years with technology. Robots can now take care of us.

  a memory   b method   c progress

6 Computers and apps can now _____ sentences into many different languages.

  a communicate   b translate   c method

5 Use the phrases in the box to replace the **bold** words.

ancient cultures	making progress
communicates well in	good method
my number one goal	bad memory

1 I am not **improving** in my studies. I wish I was doing better at school. _____

2 Many **people from the past** built amazing buildings and cities. _____

3 My sister **is very good at speaking** Arabic. She has lived in Jordan for two years. _____

4 Talking to others is a **useful practice** for improving language skills. _____

5 In the next five years, traveling the world is **the most important thing to me**. _____

6 I am not good at learning languages. I have a **difficult time remembering everything**.

_____

READING SKILL: Identifying opinions ▶11.2

1 Read the sentences. Find two opinions. Write *O* (opinion).

a   I work on the weekends. ____

b   I think I work too much. ____

c   I believe the memory of a place is better than the experience. ____

d   I have over 50 emails to reply to each day. ____

e   I communicate in English at work. ____

2 Read the sentences. Choose *Opinion* or *Fact*.

	Opinion	Fact
1 I have worked in business since 2015.	☐	☐
2 I don't even remember being there.	☐	☐
3 I believe I need to change my life.	☐	☐
4 I feel our culture tells us to be busy.	☐	☐
5 I think this quote says it all.	☐	☐

READING: Practice

3 Read the article. Is your life like the writer's? Why or why not?

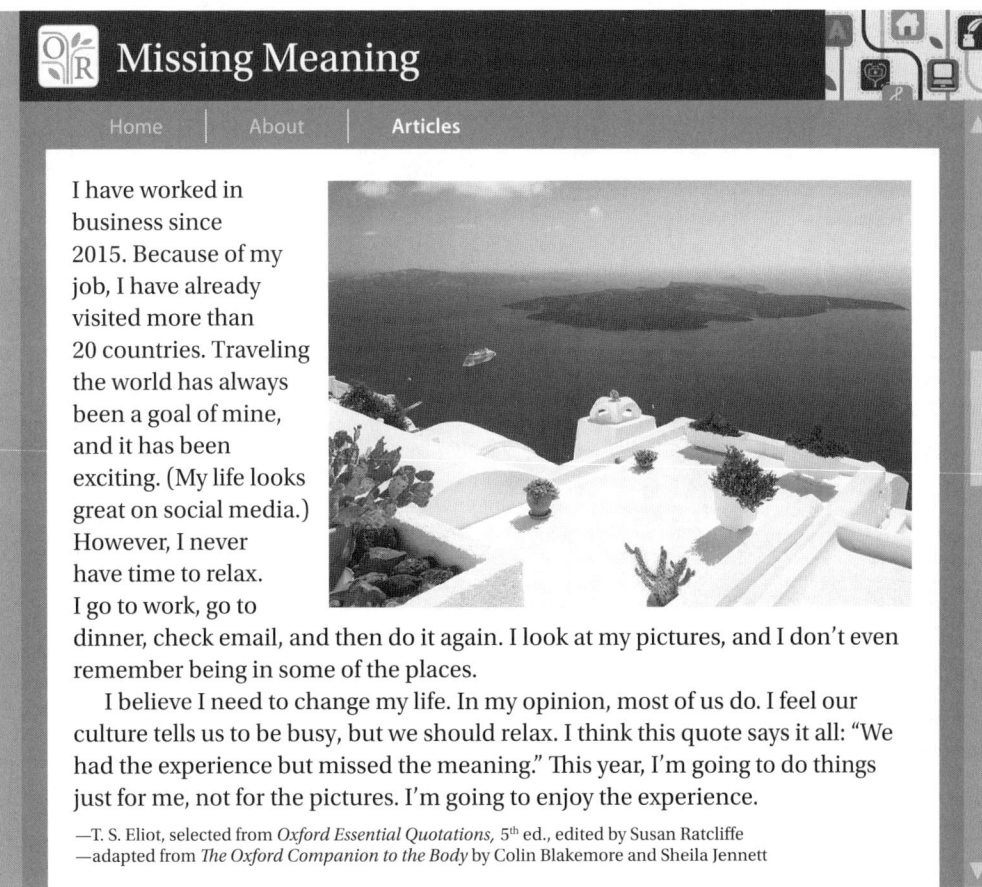

℞ Missing Meaning

| Home | About | **Articles** |

I have worked in business since 2015. Because of my job, I have already visited more than 20 countries. Traveling the world has always been a goal of mine, and it has been exciting. (My life looks great on social media.) However, I never have time to relax. I go to work, go to dinner, check email, and then do it again. I look at my pictures, and I don't even remember being in some of the places.

I believe I need to change my life. In my opinion, most of us do. I feel our culture tells us to be busy, but we should relax. I think this quote says it all: "We had the experience but missed the meaning." This year, I'm going to do things just for me, not for the pictures. I'm going to enjoy the experience.

—T. S. Eliot, selected from *Oxford Essential Quotations,* 5th ed., edited by Susan Ratcliffe
—adapted from *The Oxford Companion to the Body* by Colin Blakemore and Sheila Jennett

4 Correct the incorrect sentences.

1   The writer has visited more than 30 countries.

_____

2   It has always been the writer's goal to be in business.

_____

3   The writer enjoys looking at her pictures and remembering the experience.

_____

4   The writer thinks everyone needs to change their lives.

_____

5   The writer thinks traveling for her job is relaxing.

_____

5 Complete the sentences with words from the reading.

1   The writer thinks her life has been _____. It looks good on _____.

2   The writer never has time to _____.

3   The writer goes to work, eats dinner, checks email, and does _____.

4   The writer thinks our culture tells us to be _____.

5   This year the writer plans to enjoy the _____.

6   The quote says, "We had the _____ but missed the _____."

6 Does the writer agree with the sentences? Choose *Yes* or *No*.

		Yes	No
1	Being busy is great.	☐	☐
2	Taking pictures is very important.	☐	☐
3	Relaxing should be part of our culture.	☐	☐
4	Work is the most meaningful part of life.	☐	☐
5	When you go somewhere beautiful, it's always a great time.	☐	☐
6	Social media doesn't tell the whole story.	☐	☐

REAL-WORLD ENGLISH: Making, accepting, and refusing offers ▶11.4

1 🎧 Complete the dialogue from parts of the video with the correct words.

Andy: ¹_____ you like some breakfast?

Max: ²_____, thanks.

Andy: Hey, Max, I have an idea. I can lend you some money for a ticket to Japan. You could pay me back this summer.

Max: That's very ³_____ of you … ⁴_____ … it's OK. I can stay here. I can draw!

Andy: That sounds like a good idea.

Max: Oh, have you seen my phone charger? I need to call my mum.

Andy: Uh, no, ⁵_____. But you can use ⁶_____

Max: Great, ⁷_____!

2 Are the phrases used to make, accept, or refuse an offer?

		Make	Accept	Refuse
1	That would be great.	☐	☐	☐
2	That's OK. I'm fine.	☐	☐	☐
3	Would you like anything to drink?	☐	☐	☐
4	That's very kind of you. Thanks.	☐	☐	☐
5	You can have my seat.	☐	☐	☐
6	That's alright, but thanks.	☐	☐	☐

3 Read the conversations. Then complete the chart with the correct statements.

Conversation 1

Friend 1:   Oh no! I'm running really late now.

Friend 2:   Do you want to use my car? You'll get there faster than taking the bus.

Friend 1:   I don't know. Won't you need it?

Friend 2:   Nope, not until tonight.

Friend 1:   OK then. That would be great! Thanks so much!

Conversation 2

Colleague 1:   I can't find the email that Dan sent with the information for the meeting.

Colleague 2:   I can send it to you.

Colleague 1:   Great, thanks.

Colleague 2:   No problem.

Colleague 1:   Oh, wait. Here it is. I found it. Never mind. Thanks though.

Offer	1	*Do you want to use my car? You'll get there faster than taking the bus.*
	2	
Accept small offer	3	
Accept big offer	4	
Refuse small offer	5	
Refuse big offer	6	

LISTENING SKILL: Listening for specific information ▶11.3

1 🔊 Read the questions below. Then listen to the Unit Review Podcast. Choose the correct answers.

1   Who is Jack Vanders?
   a   a writer   b   an actor   c   a professor

2   What does Katia want to be?
   a   famous   b   a writer   c   an actor

3   What is Katia worried about?
   a   failing   b   her progress   c   performing for an audience

4   What job experience does Katia have?
   a   none   b   worked at a newspaper   c   wrote college news

5   What does Jack Vanders say?
   a   You might fail.   b   Adults don't worry.   c   You can succeed.

UNIT REVIEW: Podcast

🔘 **Go online to listen to the podcast from the Unit Review.**

2 🔊 Listen to the Unit Review Podcast again, and choose the correct answers.

1   Since Katia was *eleven / ten*, she has wanted to be a news reporter.
2   Katia has *already / not yet* written news articles.
3   Jack Vanders says every adult has *had / not had* a job they feel they might not be good at.
4   Jack Vanders encourages Katia to look at her *progress / goals*.
5   Jack Vanders thinks it *will / will not* become easier.

3 🔊 Choose the best summary of the advice from the podcast.

a   Young people can succeed with help.   ☐
b   Progress is success. Keep trying.   ☐
c   Successful adults ask a lot of questions to understand.   ☐
d   Working on a team brings the best results.   ☐

DISCUSSION BOARD PREPARATION

4 Look at the Unit 11 Review Discussion Point. Read the questions in the prompt. Label the sentence that best states the main idea.

_____

5 Does the writer agree with the quote? What example does he use to explain?

_____

_____

6 What has the writer learned from older people?

_____

Unit 11 Review Discussion Point

1   Read the quote. Do you think that older people do better work than younger people? Why or why not? Share your ideas with the class.
"Age is nothing but experience, and some of us are more experienced than others."
—selected from *The Oxford Dictionary of American Quotations*, 2nd ed., edited by Hugh Rawsom and Margaret Miner

2   What have you learned from older people, and what have you learned from people your age?

Latest: Eric Lausser
one hour ago
No, I don't think that older people do better work than younger people. I'm only 19, and I've had a lot of experience from moving different places. I have lived in different countries and had to be a part of different cultures. My experience helps me at work. I know that people from different cultures communicate in different ways, so I'm good at understanding others. An older person may not have had the same experience. So just because you're older, it doesn't make you better at work. Maybe an older person has had different experiences and is better than me at something else.
     I have learned a lot from older people. My mom taught me to be outgoing. She knew it was hard to move and make new friends. I've also learned from my friends. I see the problems they have, and I learn from talking about them.

7 What has the writer learned from younger people?

_____

8 What advice do you think the student would give to Katia from the Unit Podcast?

_____

9 Review the rubric. Use the rubric to give a score for the reply.
Give points: 0 (not successful)–10 (successful).

Writing a Discussion Board Post	Points
The post answers the questions clearly and completely.	
The post states the main idea.	
The post has clear explanations and examples.	
The writer uses present perfect correctly.	
Sentences are complete and have correct punctuation.	
The post is long enough (100–150 words).	
Total	

WRITE YOUR POST

10 Read the quote. Do you think that older people do better work than younger people? Why or why not? Share your ideas with the class.

"Age is nothing but experience, and some of us are more experienced than others."
—selected from *The Oxford Dictionary of American Quotations*, 2nd ed., edited by Hugh Rawsom and Margaret Miner

11 Use the rubric from Exercise 9 to score your post. Then improve your post.

 Go online to add your comments to the discussion board.

12 Change

1 Match the beginning of the sentence in A with the ending in B to make sentences on weather change.

A

1 When it rains, ____
2 If it's cloudy, ____
3 When the sun comes out, ____
4 If there's no rain, ____
5 When it gets very cold, ____

B

a it may rain.
b sometimes there is snow.
c the river level rises.
d the grass and plants die.
e it feels warmer.

2 Write the commas in the correct places.

1 When people change jobs they often get nervous.
2 If people have too many changes in their lives they find it difficult to feel safe.
3 When people are busy they feel better.
4 If people have friends they can talk about changes and get help.
5 When big changes happen it takes a while to feel OK again.

3 Correct the incorrect sentences.

1 If people use fossil fuels, climate change gets worse.

_____

2 When people use solar power, it be better for the environment.

_____

3 When garbage gets into the water, it not safe to drink.

_____

4 When the temperature of the sea changes some plants die.

_____

First conditional ▶12.2

4 Complete the sentences with a verb from the box. Use the first conditional.

change	have	know	~~need~~	see

1 If I move, I ___will need___ to find a new job.
2 If I get a new job, I _____ anyone at work. I guess I'll meet new people.
3 If I become friends with Susan, I _____ a lot of fun. She is really funny!
4 If I go to school abroad, I _____ my family for a year. I will really miss them!
5 If I get married, my life _____. My wife and I will move to Thailand for her job.

5 Join the pairs of sentences. Use the first conditional.

1 We graduate in June. We need jobs soon.
   If we graduate in June, we'll need jobs soon.
2 I learn Mandarin. I go to China for a year.

_____

3 My brother lives with me. We share the cost of the apartment.

_____

4 I don't do well on the test. I pass the class.

_____

5 I don't learn to relax. I enjoy life.

_____

6 Rewrite the sentences. Correct the mistakes in the first conditional.

1 If I bike to work, I feel better.
   If I bike to work, I'll feel better.
2 If I eat more vegetables, I'I be healthier.

_____

3 If I get together with friends tonight I will have more fun.

_____

4 If you sleeps more, you won't be so tired in class.

_____

Climate change ▶12.1

1 Match the comments with the descriptions in the box.

~~reduce garbage~~	protect the environment
stay safe in a storm	temperatures increase
climate change	sea levels rise

1 "Don't throw away boxes and other things you can use again." ___reduce garbage___

2 "Take care of the plants and animals in our world." _____

3 "Move away from windows. Don't drive. Stay where you are." _____

4 "In the summer, it gets very hot here." _____

5 "Temperatures and weather are changing in places all over the world." _____

6 "Ice in Antarctica and Greenland turns to water, and the oceans get bigger." _____

2 For each pair, write *S* (similar) or *D* (different).

_____ 1 climate / weather

_____ 2 increase / reduce

_____ 3 environment / world

_____ 4 rise / reduce

_____ 5 storm / hurricane

_____ 6 increase / rise

VOCABULARY DEVELOPMENT: Noun suffixes: -tion, -ment ▶12.2

3 Are the suffixes correct? Choose *Yes* or *No*.

		Yes	No
1	Do I need to correction my paper?	☐	☐
2	The government makes laws to protect the environment.	☐	☐
3	I management four people at work.	☐	☐
4	I didn't understand the instructions.	☐	☐
5	Do you agreement with me?	☐	☐
6	Does that measuretion look correct?	☐	☐

4 Make nouns from the verbs in the box using the suffixes to complete the chart.

excite	~~instruct~~ manage protect

instruction	-tion
	-ment

5 Complete the sentences using the nouns from the chart in Exercise 4.

1 The _____ at my office is really good. They support all the workers and really help them.

2 Technology has changed our world, but the classroom hasn't. _____ is the same.

3 If you are in a sunny climate, you need _____ from the sun!

4 Some change is good. Change can make life more interesting. For many, it causes _____.

Airplane travel ▶12.3

6 Unscramble the letters to make words about air travel.

1 snepsraseg _____

2 gualgeg _____

3 tiplo _____

4 okob a gfitlh _____

5 tgea _____

7 Complete the sentences with a word or phrase from Exercise 6.

1 Oh no! We are at the wrong _____. Our plane is leaving from G4!

2 Please be quiet. I can't hear the _____. I think he is talking about the flight.

3 There are too many _____ on the plane. I was hoping for a seat, but I don't think I'll get one.

4 You can only bring two bags on the plane. Can you reduce your _____?

5 Can you help me _____? You always find the best prices for plane tickets.

READING SKILL: Using visuals and data ▶12.1

1 Look at the infographic. Complete the sentences with words from the box.

| Brazil | forests | hectares | loss | places | the United States |

1 The infographic shows the _____ of _____.

2 The infographic shows _____ in the world that are losing forests.

3 The loss of forests is measured in _____.

4 The country with the greatest loss is _____.

5 The country with the smallest loss is _____.

2 Look at the infographic and photo. Choose *True* or *False*.

	True	False
1 The photo shows the loss of forests.	☐	☐
2 The smallest loss of forests is about 500,000 hectares.	☐	☐
3 The biggest loss of forests is about 3,500,000 hectares.	☐	☐
4 The text will say animals lose their habitats.	☐	☐
5 The text will discuss causes and effects.	☐	☐

READING: Practice

3 Read the article. What does the Sierra Club do?

Make a Difference with the Sierra Club

Home | About | **Articles**

Population growth has many effects. One is that forests are cut down for land to grow food for the increasing population. When forests are cut down, animals and plants lose their habitats. Some will die. However, the story doesn't have to end there. In 1892, businessmen and professors from San Francisco Bay created the Sierra Club to protect forests and other parts of the Sierra Nevada Mountains in the United States. Now more than 1.4 million people are a part of it. The goals of the organization have increased. The Sierra Club works to reduce the use of fossil fuels, protect the country's waters, and respond to climate change by creating habitats for plants, animals, and people. When people join together, they have more power. They can create real change. We can protect forests and our environment. You can help us change the world's story. Join today.

—adapted from *The Oxford Encyclopedia of the History of American Science, Medicine, and Technology,* edited by Hugh Richard Slotten

Loss of Forests

Land in Hectares (in millions) (a unit of area equal to 10,000 square meters)

4,000,000
3,500,000
3,000,000
2,500,000
2,000,000
1,500,000
1,000,000
500,000
0

Brazil Indonesia Russian Fed. Mexico Papua New Guinea Peru United States

Countries

4 What is the purpose of the text? Choose two purposes.

a To get the United States to do more to protect oceans ☐

b To get people to join the Sierra Club ☐

c To show that people can have an effect on the environment ☐

d To get people to reduce their use of fossil fuels ☐

5 Match the questions with the answers.

_____ 1 Who started the Sierra Club?

_____ 2 When was it started?

_____ 3 What was its first goal?

_____ 4 How many people belong now?

a 1.4 million

b protect forests

c 1892

d businessmen and professors

6 Correct the incorrect sentences.

1 The goals of the organization have decreased since it began.

_____

2 The organization works to reduce fossil fuels.

_____

3 Part of the problem is we need land to grow food.

_____

4 The writer wants people to act on their own to create change.

_____

5 The loss of forests does not mean the loss of habitats.

_____

REAL-WORLD ENGLISH: Agreeing and disagreeing with opinions ▶12.4

1 🔘 Watch the video. Choose *True* or *False*.

		True	False
1	Andy tells Max he got the internship, and Max is disappointed.	☐	☐
2	Max agrees that Andy can't take a vacation.	☐	☐
3	Andy thinks that he should take some time off.	☐	☐
4	Max tells Andy to ask for the time off.	☐	☐
5	In the end, Andy agrees to ask for the time off.	☐	☐

2 Order the dialogue.

Hyun

____ It's not going to be late. Flights take off in the snow. I really don't want to miss it.

____ I think we should run. I want to make it to the gate on time!

____ OK, you walk fast, and I'll run. I'll meet you at the gate!

Amber

____ Miss it? If it's late, they'll tell us. I'm not going to run, but I'll walk faster.

____ Oh, OK, Hyun. I'll see you there. I really think we'll be OK.

____ Uh, I don't know. I don't think we have to. It's snowing. I think the flight will be late.

3 Read the chart. Then compete the dialogue using the phrases of agreeing and disagreeing with opinions.

	Fernando	Luis
Wants to get a job	Yes	No
Wants to be roommates	Yes	No
Likes the class	Yes	Yes
Wants to work together for class	Yes	Yes

Fernando: We need money. We should get jobs.

Luis: ¹_____. We do need money, but we also need time to study.

Fernando: We could save money if we became roommates! What do you think?

Luis: ²_____. I'm going away for the break so I'll be gone for part of the semester.

Fernando: That reminds me. I think that film class next semester with Professor Jeffries looks really good.

Luis: ³_____.

Fernando: In the class, you get to make a movie. I think we could make something cool.

Luis: ⁴_____.

UNIT REVIEW: Podcast

Go online to listen to the podcast from the Unit Review.

1 Listen to the Unit Review Podcast. Put the events in the correct order (1–4). One event will not be used.

_____ Matt wishes his mom "Happy birthday."

_____ Matt reads the airport announcement that planes may be delayed.

_____ The news reporter asks Matt to tell his story.

_____ Matt's gate is changed.

_____ Matt shares the text message that his flight is canceled.

2 Listen again. Choose *True*, *False*, or *Not Given*.

		True	False	Not Given
1	Matt didn't sleep.	☐	☐	☐
2	There was a lot of snow and ice.	☐	☐	☐
3	Matt flies a lot.	☐	☐	☐
4	Matt's mom thinks change can make you happier.	☐	☐	☐
5	Matt's mom will have to pick him up at 2 a.m.	☐	☐	☐

LISTENING SKILL: Identifying levels of formality ▶12.3

3 Listen to the sentences. Which sentences are formal? Which sentences are informal?

	Formal	Informal
1	☐	☐
2	☐	☐
3	☐	☐
4	☐	☐
5	☐	☐

DISCUSSION BOARD PREPARATION

4 Look at the Unit 12 Review Discussion Point. Read the questions in the prompt. Label the sentences that best state the main idea.

_____

5 What examples does the writer use to explain things that change in life?

_____

6 Does the writer think change is always a good thing? Why or why not?

_____

Unit 12 Review Discussion Point

1   Read the quote. What kinds of things change in life? Is change always a good thing?
    "To live is to change, and to be perfect is to have changed often."
    —John Henry Newman, selected from *Oxford Essential Quotations*, 5ᵗʰ ed., edited by Susan Ratcliffe
2   How does *change* change you?

Latest: **Nell Hobbs**
one hour ago
Everything in life changes! Your friends change, and the music you like changes. Your gate at the airport and the time of your flight change. Then there are bigger changes that affect the world, like climate change and storms. I don't think change is always good because climate change is destroying our environment.
    I don't think change is good or bad. It's just part of life. Avoiding change is really not an option. If you expect change, it won't be so bad. In my opinion, change can change you because you experience something new. You might love it. You might hate it. You learn how you feel. You might even change the way you think about something. But I think to really change, you have to be open to it. You have to want to learn something. If not, then you'll probably stay the same.

7 What's one way that change can change you in a good way?

_____

8 Do you think the student agrees with Matt's mom's advice from the Unit Podcast? Why or why not?

_____

_____

9 Review the rubric. Use the rubric to give a score for the reply.
     Give points: 0 (not successful)–10 (successful).

Writing a Discussion Board Post	Points
The post answers the questions clearly and completely.	
The post states the main idea.	
The post has clear explanations and examples.	
The writer uses the zero and first conditional correctly.	
The writer uses the correct noun suffixes *-ment* and *-tion*.	
The post is long enough (100–150 words).	
Total	

WRITE YOUR POST

10 Read the quote. What kinds of things change in life? Is change always a good thing?

     "To live is to change, and to be perfect is to have changed often."
     —John Henry Newman, selected from *Oxford Essential Quotations*, 5ᵗʰ ed.,
     edited by Susan Ratcliffe

11 Use the rubric from Exercise 9 to score your post. Then improve your post.

 Go online to add your comments to the discussion board.